Forms for Behavior Analysis with Children

Joseph R. Cautela
Julie Cautela
Sharon Esonis

RESEARCH PRESS
2612 North Mattis Avenue
Champaign, Illinois 61822

To our own children . . .

Joseph R. Cautela, Jr.	Tory J. Cautela	Patrick J. Esonis
Robert J. Cautela	and	
John J. Cautela	Markanthony J. Cautela	
Carol A. Cautela Landers		
and		
Christopher J. Cautela		

. . . this work is lovingly dedicated.

12 11 10 9 8   99 00 01 02 03

Printed in the United States of America.

Copies of this book may be ordered from the publisher at the address given on the title page.

Composition by Omegatype Typography, Inc.
Cover design by Jack W. Davis

ISBN 0-87822-267-7
Library of Congress Catalog Number 82-62572

Contents

Foreword

The diagnosis, assessment, and treatment of childhood disorders and problem behaviors recently have received increased attention in clinical practice and research. The more explicit recognition and delineation of childhood disorders in the *Diagnostic and Statistical Manual of Mental Disorders* (DSM III) relative to previous diagnostic systems and the emergence of books and journals on childhood treatment within clinical psychology and behavior therapy attest to the development of child clinical work. Despite increased activity in this area, a paucity of information exists to aid clinical practice. The present book makes a major contribution by providing a variety of assessment devices and diagnostic and treatment recommendations for use in clinical work with children and adolescents.

The book includes and elaborates upon a large number of measures that are likely to be of considerable use in assessing children's problems and in generating concrete treatment prescriptions. But it is not merely a compilation or catalogue of these measures. Because the assessment devices are designed for clinical use, details rarely available in other sources are presented. For instance, details of administration and specific treatments that might accompany a particular pattern of performance are nicely codified. Also, different assessment methods are compared and evaluated so that the clinician will be able to make judgments about the appropriate set of devices that is likely to yield the maximum information in each case.

A highlight of the book is the breadth of coverage reflected in the measures. Different clinical problems are represented, including anxiety, poor social skills, and somatic complaints. The different perspectives relevant to child assessment also are sampled, including measures for parents, children, teachers, and therapists. Related information about child performance in different settings such as the home and school is included. Finally, different assessment formats are encompassed, ranging from direct observations and interviews to informant ratings and self-report.

The measures are designed to provide a comprehensive portrait of childhood problems with an eye to how the information can be used to design behavioral treatments. Thus, special attention is devoted to assessment of reinforcing and aversive consequences and to the wide range of activities that are important to the child and might be incorporated into treatment. But besides being useful in clinical work, this collection of assessment measures is likely to generate important research as well. By providing a systematic way of collecting data on children, the measures are likely to prompt research in behavioral assessment. Apart from psychometric work on specific measures, the interrelationship of different measures, target problems, assessment perspectives, and treatment could advance the field considerably. Overall, the collection of measures and recommendations provided by Cautela, Cautela, and Esonis reflects extensive clinical experience in the assessment and treatment of childhood disorders. The book should be quite valuable to practitioners and to those who wish to investigate childhood disorders.

University of Pittsburgh School of Medicine
Alan E. Kazdin
Professor of Child Psychology and Psychology

Preface

Diagnosis, in the traditional sense, is not directly related to the treatment process; thus, within the behavioral model, the term *behavioral assessment* is employed rather than *diagnosis*. Behavioral assessment involves describing the topography of the target response and discovering the antecedents and consequences that influence it. The first step is to operationalize the target response. Then the duration, intensity, latency, and frequency of the target response are recorded, as well as the antecedents and consequences. After the initial behavioral assessment is completed, a treatment program is devised; but it is important to note that behavioral assessment should be constantly occurring during the course of treatment. The treatment procedure can then be evaluated on a continual basis and modified according to the assessment feedback.

There are a number of sources for behavioral assessment, which include:

1. Direct observation
2. Interviews with significant others
3. Interviews with the client
4. Case histories provided by other therapists (The information provided by therapists espousing a nonbehavioral model is often not useful to behavioral assessment. However, this doesn't preclude the responsibility to scrutinize the case data for possible cues that could be helpful.)
5. Behavioral forms or inventories (By behavioral forms or inventories we mean systematized data-gathering forms to be filled out by the client, therapist, or significant others.)

In my years of clinical practice, during which I have treated many children, I have found it economical, heuristic, and facilitating to employ forms to obtain relevant information for the treatment of particular target behaviors. It is my assumption that the target response is embedded in the total life situation of the client. Therefore, some forms involve questions that are not specific to the particular target response, e.g., the Behavior Analysis History Questionnaire, Bodily Cues for Tension and Anxiety, or certain reinforcement questionnaires. There are also questionnaires that are designed to obtain information for a specific target response, e.g., the Fear Inventory or the Physical Complaint Survey Schedule. Since an assumption of the behavioral model is that the total environment affects any client behavior, forms have been designed to obtain information from a wide variety of sources, such as institutional staff, school personnel, parents, and significant others, as well as the therapist.

An important difference between the assessment of adults and the assessment of children is that, in many instances, the children's self-reports are inaccurate because of a lack of skills due to chronological age or handicaps such as retardation or autism. This has resulted in the development of more forms to be filled out by significant others and the oral administration of the forms by the therapist.

While working as behavioral clinicians, my coauthors and I have developed various methods of assessing children and significant others in the child's life; we have been able to discriminate for our purposes what questions should be asked of whom and when, and have formulated guidelines for specific and general situations. We have found in our practice that standardizing these components saves clinical time and provides systematic methods for proceeding with clients. Since these forms are so helpful in our own work, we offer them here so that others might benefit from them as well.

For simplicity's sake, the term *therapist* is used throughout this book to refer to the person administering the forms and conducting the interventions; however, many other professionals will find this book useful as well. We have attempted to explain the optimal use of the forms in some detail, so that professionals in a variety of settings and at different levels of understanding of behavior modification might be able to successfully identify overt and covert events germane to the problems of the child or adolescent. These forms were collected in the hope that they would assist school personnel, counselors, child therapists, and pediatricians in helping parents and children; they also may be helpful in a therapeutic supervisory situation for both the supervisor and the trainee.

One important point deserves mention. These forms should be regarded as more than just assessment instruments; they can also be prescriptive tools, since they can provide cues for appropriate behavior. By stating individual behaviors in the positive rather than in the negative, the forms suggest adaptive behavior and appropriate behavior patterns to incorporate into a client's repertoire.

Finally, the forms presented in this manual were developed in collaboration with Julie Cautela and Sharon Esonis. Their extensive experience with children and adolescents was especially valuable in presenting information on the rationale and use of the forms, which, together with the related readings and bibliography, make a unique contribution to this manual.

JOSEPH R. CAUTELA, Ph.D.

Introduction

The forms included in this book have been arranged according to the phase in treatment in which they are most commonly used. There are three main categories: Intake Packet, which covers the most general forms which are probably applicable to every entering client; Intervention Development, which encompasses those forms used for pinpointing target behaviors, discovering reinforcers, and recording baseline data; and Intervention Recording and Guidelines, which includes forms for ongoing recording of client progress and guidelines for specific procedures.

Each form title is followed by a capital letter in parentheses. The letter indicates the person who is to complete the form, as follows:

C = child
A = adolescent
P = parent
S = school personnel
T = therapist

The Guidelines for Time-out and Parental Discipline are not to be filled in, and thus have no letters. If there are several letters with an *and,* there is a different version of the form for each person. If there is an *or,* several different people may be asked to fill out the same form.

Each form is preceded by an introduction, which is intended to familiarize the reader with the purpose, content, and uses of the form. It begins with the Rationale/Purpose section, in which the purpose and design of the form are explained. This is followed by an Administration section that tells the reader who is to complete the form and how it is best administered. Next is the Guidelines section, which gives detailed information on the administration of the form and on issues related to the form's structure or content. The Item Breakdown section categorizes all items so the therapist can quickly see what content areas are included. This is followed by the Use of the Information section, where the data are interpreted and related to treatment. The Comparison to Other Forms section lists other forms that have related information and suggests possible comparisons of certain data, while the Recommended Readings section gives other sources of information on topics relevant to the target behavior and its treatment.

The following table illustrates the use of the forms from general assessment to specific assessment to intervention. Forms listed under each group provide information either to be used by that group to intervene or with that group for treatment. For example, parents do not fill out the Response Cost Survey Schedule, but the information from that schedule can be very useful in the parent intervention process.

THERAPIST
General Assessment
Behavior Analysis History Questionnaire
(P, with an Addendum for Adolescents, and A)
Behavior Status Checklist
(P, with an Addendum for Adolescents, C, and A)
Reinforcement Survey Schedules
(C and A)

PARENT	SCHOOL PERSONNEL	THERAPIST	CHILD
Specific Assessment	**Specific Assessment**	**Specific Assessment**	**Specific Assessment**
Parents' and Children's Reinforcement Survey Schedule (P, C, and A)	School Behavior Status Checklist (S, with an Addendum for Adolescents)	Behavior Record Form (P, T, or S)	Assertive Behavior Survey Schedule (C and A)
Response Cost Survey Schedule (C and A)	School Reinforcement Survey Schedule (C and A)	Home Visit Observation Form (T)	Bodily Cues for Tension and Anxiety (C and A)
Behavior Record Form (P, T, or S)	Behavior Record Form (P, T, or S)	**Intervention** Behavioral Rating Card (S)	Fear Inventory (C and A)
Intervention Guidelines for Parental Discipline	Home Visit Observation Form (T)	Guidelines for Parental Discipline	Medical History Inventory (P)
Guidelines for Time-out	**Intervention** Behavioral Rating Card (S)	Guidelines for Time-out	Physical Complaint Survey Schedule (C and A)
Progress Chart (C and A)	Guidelines for Time-out	Motivation Assessment of Parents and Children (T)	Self-Evaluation Scale (C and A)
	Progress Chart (C and A)	Progress Chart (C and A)	Parents' and Children's Reinforcement Survey Schedule (P, C, and A)
		Session Report (T)	Reinforcement Menu (C and A)
			Response Cost Survey Schedule (C and A)
			Intervention Behavioral Rating Card (S)
			Progress Chart (C and A)

2

Intake Packet

BEHAVIOR ANALYSIS HISTORY QUESTIONNAIRE (P and A)

RATIONALE/PURPOSE

A primary form in the client's intake folder should be the Behavior Analysis History Questionnaire (Forms P and A). This form, once filled out, will contain basic important information on past history. It should not take the place of the initial interview, but it does save the therapist time in listing details such as number of siblings, names of previous therapists (if any), past and current family information, and the medical, educational, and religious history of the client.

There is an Addendum for Adolescents which includes a job history and a section for identifying certain negative self-statements that would indicate a need for immediate intervention, e.g., "Life is hopeless" or "I feel like killing myself."

ADMINISTRATION

Only the parents are asked to fill out the Behavior Analysis History Questionnaire for a child's presenting complaint, since most of the items are dates and other background information. Each parent should complete a copy, to allow comparison of parental perspectives. However, in treating adolescents, it is best to have both the parents and the adolescent fill out separate forms of the Behavior Analysis History Questionnaire. The comparison of parental and adolescent statements may provide insight into different perceptions between the two, e.g., comparing the answers to questions such as "How do you and your spouse get along?" and "How do your mother and father get along?"

As part of the Intake Packet, the Behavior Analysis History Questionnaire is given to the client and/or parent at the end of the first session. It is to be completed at home in time for the second session.

GUIDELINES

1. It is usually helpful for the therapist to review the Behavior Analysis History Questionnaire before the third session and to highlight any particular areas or items she may want to take up with the client for clarification or possible treatment.
2. It also is helpful to review this questionnaire immediately before making a home visit, since it contains so much information on the family.

ITEM BREAKDOWN

FORM P
   I. General Information
  II. Referral Information
 III. Family Information
  IV. Educational History
   V. Medical History
  VI. Religious History
 VII. Other Information
       ADDENDUM FOR ADOLESCENTS
VIII. Negative Thoughts
       (indicating need for
       immediate intervention)
  IX. Job History

FORM A

USE OF THE INFORMATION

Since this is one of the first forms given, discussion of the answers to questions on the Behavior Analysis History Questionnaire may elicit much related and helpful information on current environmental cues. Behavioral analysis focuses on the present, but past experiences that may provide information on the present problem are not neglected.

It is often helpful to refer back to the Behavior Analysis History Questionnaire during the course of treatment for particular details or reminders of the client's general history and environment or as an indication of the original baseline of the presenting complaint. This form is also a starting point for giving the client other, more specialized, forms.

COMPARISON TO OTHER FORMS

The Behavior Analysis History Questionnaire is related to a wide variety of other inventories in that it serves to further identify forms that would be appropriate to administer.

RECOMMENDED READINGS

Cautela, J. R. Behavior Analysis History Questionnaire. In *Behavior analysis forms for clinical intervention.* Champaign, Ill.: Research Press, 1977.

Marholin II, D., & Bijou, S. Behavioral assessment: Listen when the data speak. In D. Marholin II (Ed.), *Child behavior therapy.* New York: Gardner Press, 1978.

Wolpe, J. A Life History Questionnaire. In *Psychotherapy by reciprocal inhibition.* Stanford, Calif.: Stanford University Press, 1958.

BEHAVIOR ANALYSIS HISTORY QUESTIONNAIRE (P)

I. GENERAL INFORMATION

Name _____ Date _____

Name of child _____ Sex _____

Age _____ Date of birth _____

School _____ Grade _____

Address _____

_____

Telephone number _____

Marital status of parents _____

If divorced or separated, for what reason? _____

_____

Who does the child live with? _____

List brothers and sisters of the child.

Name	Sex	Age	Living at home (yes or no)
_____	_____	_____	_____
_____	_____	_____	_____
_____	_____	_____	_____
_____	_____	_____	_____
_____	_____	_____	_____

List other people who are living in the same household as the child.

Name	Sex	Age	Relationship to child (if any)
_____	_____	_____	_____
_____	_____	_____	_____
_____	_____	_____	_____
_____	_____	_____	_____

II. REFERRAL INFORMATION

Who referred you? _____

_____

What present problems (maladaptive behaviors) does the child have that indicate help is needed?

Behavior	Times occurs per week/per month
_____	_____
_____	_____
_____	_____

What do you think is presently causing these behaviors? _____

_____

_____

Have you sought treatment before?   Yes _____   No _____

If so, list the names of the therapists and dates of therapy in chronological order.

Name of therapist   *Dates seen*

_____   _____

_____   _____

_____   _____

III. FAMILY INFORMATION

Mother

Name _____ Age _____

Height _____ ft. _____ in. Weight _____ lbs.

Religion _____

Occupation _____

What activities does mother do with the child? _____

_____

How does mother punish the child? _____

_____

What does she punish? _____

_____

How does mother reward the child? _____

_____

What does she reward? _____

_____

How would the child describe his or her mother? _____

_____

How does the child get along with his or her mother? _____

_____

Does mother favor any one child? Yes _____ No _____ If so, who and why? _____

_____

Father

Name _____ Age _____

Height _____ ft. _____ in. Weight _____ lbs.

Religion _____

Occupation _____

What activities does father do with the child? _____

_____

How does father punish the child? _____

_____

What does he punish? _____

_____

How does father reward the child? _____

_____

What does he reward? _____

_____

How would the child describe his or her father? _____

How does the child get along with his or her father? _____

Does father favor any one child?   Yes _____   No _____   If so, who and why? _____

How do you and your spouse get along?

Poorly _____   Fairly well _____   Well _____   Excellently _____

Child

Has any previous psychological testing been done? If so, please indicate tests, approximate dates of administration, and results.

Test	*Date*	*Results*
_____	_____	_____
_____	_____	_____
_____	_____	_____

List the child's interests and hobbies. _____

_____

_____

_____

IV. EDUCATIONAL HISTORY

	Name of school	*Location*	*Dates*	*Grades normally earned*
Nursery	_____	_____	_____	_____
Grammar	_____	_____	_____	_____
	_____	_____	_____	_____
Secondary	_____	_____	_____	_____
	_____	_____	_____	_____

How well does the child adjust to school situations?

Poorly _____   Fairly well _____   Well _____   Excellently _____

List any significant events relating to school that you think have a bearing on the child's present problems.

_____

_____

_____

_____

How would you describe the child's performance in school? _____

Has any previous educational testing been done? If so, please indicate tests, approximate dates of administration, and results.

Test	*Date*	*Results*
_____	_____	_____
_____	_____	_____
_____	_____	_____

V. MEDICAL HISTORY

List any childhood diseases the child has had. _____

_____

_____

List any operations the child has had. _____

_____

List any significant illnesses the child has had. _____

_____

List any physical ailments the child presently has. _____

_____

When was the last time the child had a complete physical exam? _____

What were the results? _____

What drugs is the child presently taking and why? _____

_____

VI. RELIGIOUS HISTORY

In what religion is the child being raised?

Protestant _____ Catholic _____ Jewish _____ Other _____

Does the child receive religious instruction? Yes _____ No _____ If so, where? _____

Do you and/or your spouse regularly attend religious services? Yes _____ No _____

VII. OTHER INFORMATION

Please add anything you feel might help in understanding your child's problem. _____

_____

_____

_____

_____

ADDENDUM FOR ADOLESCENTS

VIII. NEGATIVE THOUGHTS

If your adolescent child has ever expressed any of these thoughts, put a check mark in the column that best describes the frequency of their occurrence.

	Not at all	Sometimes	A lot
Life is hopeless.			
I'm lonely.			
The future is hopeless.			
Nobody cares about me.			
I feel like killing myself.			
I'm a failure.			
I'm dumb.			
People usually don't like me.			
I'm going to faint.			
I'm going to have a panic attack.			
Other negative thoughts your adolescent may have:			
_____			
_____			
_____			

IX. JOB HISTORY

List the jobs your adolescent child has held and their dates. Then note which aspects of each job were the most pleasurable, e.g., working with people or doing a particular type of work, and which aspects were the most anxiety-provoking or troublesome.

Dates	Job title	Salary	Liked	Disliked
_____	_____	_____	_____	_____
_____	_____	_____	_____	_____
_____	_____	_____	_____	_____
_____	_____	_____	_____	_____
_____	_____	_____	_____	_____

How often did he or she miss work?

a. As a general estimate for all jobs _____

b. For the jobs enjoyed _____

c. For the jobs disliked _____

How did he or she get along with fellow employees?

Not at all _____ Fairly well _____ Very well _____

What bothered him or her most about fellow employees? _____

_____

How did he or she get along with supervisors? _____

_____

What bothered him or her about supervisors? _____

What training or education has he or she had in occupational skills? (List on-the-job training as well as course work.) _____

_____

_____

_____

What job, if any, is he or she presently holding? _____

Does it satisfy him or her intellectually?   Yes _____   No _____

Emotionally?   Yes _____   No _____   Physically?   Yes _____   No _____

What ambitions does he or she have at the present time? _____

_____

BEHAVIOR ANALYSIS HISTORY QUESTIONNAIRE (A)

I. GENERAL INFORMATION

Name _____ Date _____

Age _____ Date of birth _____ Sex _____

School _____ Grade _____

Address _____

_____

Telephone number _____

Marital status of parents _____

If divorced or separated, for what reason? _____

_____

Who do you live with? _____

List your brothers and sisters.

Name	Sex	Age	Living at home (yes or no)

List other people who are living in the household with you.

Name	Sex	Age	Relationship to you (if any)

II. REFERRAL INFORMATION

Who referred you? _____

_____

What present problems (maladaptive behaviors) do you have that indicate help is needed?

Behavior	Times occurs per week/per month

What do you think is presently causing these behaviors? _____

_____

_____

Have you sought treatment before?   Yes _____   No _____

If so, list the names of the therapists and dates of therapy in chronological order.

III. FAMILY INFORMATION

Mother

Name _____ Age _____

Height _____ ft. _____ in. Weight _____ lbs.

Religion _____

Occupation _____

What activities does your mother do with you? _____

_____

How does your mother punish you? _____

_____

What does she punish? _____

_____

How does your mother reward you? _____

_____

What does she reward? _____

_____

How would you describe your mother? _____

_____

How do you get along with your mother? _____

_____

Does your mother favor any one child? Yes _____ No _____ If so, who and why? _____

_____

Father

Name _____ Age _____

Height _____ ft. _____ in. Weight _____ lbs.

Religion _____

Occupation _____

What activities does your father do with you? _____

_____

How does your father punish you? _____

_____

What does he punish? _____

_____

How does your father reward you? _____

_____

What does he reward? _____

_____

How would you describe your father? _____

_____

How do you get along with your father? _____

_____

Does your father favor any one child? Yes _____ No _____ If so, who and why? _____

_____

How do your mother and father get along?

Poorly _____ Fairly well _____ Well _____ Excellently _____

Yourself

Have you had any previous psychological testing? If so, please indicate tests, approximate dates of administration, and results.

Test	*Date*	*Results*
_____	_____	_____
_____	_____	_____
_____	_____	_____

List your interests and hobbies. _____

_____

_____

_____

IV. EDUCATIONAL HISTORY

	Name of school	*Location*	*Dates*	*Grades normally earned*
Nursery	_____	_____	_____	_____
Grammar	_____	_____	_____	_____
	_____	_____	_____	_____
Secondary	_____	_____	_____	_____
	_____	_____	_____	_____

How well do you adjust to school situations?

Poorly _____ Fairly well _____ Well _____ Excellently _____

List any significant events relating to school that you think have a bearing on your present problems.

_____

_____

_____

_____

How would you describe your performance in school? _____

_____

Have you had any previous educational testing? If so, please indicate tests, approximate dates of administration, and results.

Test	*Date*	*Results*
_____	_____	_____
_____	_____	_____
_____	_____	_____

V. MEDICAL HISTORY

List any childhood diseases you have had. _____

_____

List any operations you have had. _____

_____

List any significant illnesses you have had. _____

_____

List any physical ailments you presently have. _____

_____

When was the last time you had a complete physical exam? _____

What were the results? _____

What drugs are you presently taking and why? _____

_____

VI. RELIGIOUS HISTORY

In what religion are you being raised?

Protestant _____ Catholic _____ Jewish _____ Other _____

Do you receive religious instruction? Yes _____ No _____ If so, where? _____

Do your parents regularly attend religious services? Yes _____ No _____

VII. OTHER INFORMATION

Please add anything you feel might help us in understanding you. _____

_____

_____

_____

_____

VIII. NEGATIVE THOUGHTS

If you have ever had any of these thoughts, put a check mark in the column that best describes the frequency of their occurrence.

	Not at all	Sometimes	A lot
Life is hopeless.			
I'm lonely.			
The future is hopeless.			
Nobody cares about me.			
I feel like killing myself.			
I'm a failure.			
I'm dumb.			
People usually don't like me.			
I'm going to faint.			

	Not at all	Sometimes	A lot
I'm going to have a panic attack.			
Other negative thoughts you may have:			
_____			
_____			
_____			

IX. JOB HISTORY

List the jobs you have held and their dates. Then note which aspects of each job were the most pleasurable, e.g., working with people or doing a particular type of work, and which aspects were the most anxiety-provoking or troublesome.

Dates	Job title	Salary	Liked	Disliked
_____	_____	_____	_____	_____
_____	_____	_____	_____	_____
_____	_____	_____	_____	_____
_____	_____	_____	_____	_____
_____	_____	_____	_____	_____

How often did you miss work?

a. As a general estimate for all jobs _____

b. For the jobs enjoyed _____

c. For the jobs disliked _____

How did you get along with fellow employees?

Not at all _____ Fairly well _____ Very well _____

What bothered you most about your fellow employees? _____

_____

How did you get along with your supervisors? _____

_____

What bothered you about your supervisors? _____

What training or education have you had in occupational skills? (List on-the-job training as well as course work.) _____

_____

_____

What job, if any, are you presently holding? _____

Does it satisfy you intellectually?   Yes _____   No _____

Emotionally?   Yes _____   No _____   Physically?   Yes _____   No _____

What ambitions do you have at the present time? _____

_____

BEHAVIOR STATUS CHECKLIST (P)

RATIONALE/PURPOSE

Parents sometimes find it difficult to pinpoint the behaviors of their child that are problematic. General traits such as laziness, shyness, lack of motivation, and lack of cooperation are attributed to the child in an attempt to explain or describe the dilemma. Behavioral definition of the descriptors can be a helpful start toward an understanding of the problem and toward development of a treatment plan.

The Behavior Status Checklist (P) was developed to facilitate the identification of adaptive and maladaptive behaviors and to ascertain the behaviors the parents view as important to target for change. The questions are stated in the positive, since it is essential to be aware of the child's strengths, as well as weaknesses.

ADMINISTRATION

The therapist generally oversees or explains the administration and use of this form. The optimal situation is to have each parent fill out a form separately.

GUIDELINES

1. This form is part of the Intake Packet. It can be completed by the parents for the second session or can be used by the therapist in the first session to become familiar with the child and parents.
2. It should be explained to the parents that the *Need to Change* category should be answered in terms of their feelings. Some behaviors irritate or bother parents but are not of great importance elsewhere. Such behaviors may be among the first to be addressed in order to promote a better relationship between parent and child.
3. Some typically adolescent behaviors are addressed in the Addendum for Adolescents. The decision to use the Addendum should be based on the behavioral functioning of the youngster in question, rather than on chronological age. Some 14-year-olds will not be involved in most of the behaviors described, whereas the behavior of some 10- and 11-year-olds might warrant the parents answering the questions on this addition.

ITEM BREAKDOWN

Number of questions: 72

Questions	Topic
1–4, 14	Attentional behaviors
5–8	School and extracurricular activities
9–13, 15–20, 21*, 22*, 25	Compliance behaviors
21*, 22*, 23, 24, 26–28, 30, 31, 33, 34*, 50, 68–71	Responsibility/self-control behaviors
32, 35–37	Age- and sex-appropriate behaviors
29, 38–45, 56*, 58	Adaptive/relaxed functioning
34*, 46–49, 51–56*, 57, 59–67	Social behaviors
72	Other behaviors

Number of questions: 16

Questions	Topic
73, 75*	Social behaviors
76–85, 88	Responsibility/self-control behaviors
74, 75*	Adaptive/relaxed functioning
86, 87	Sexual behaviors

*This indicates that the item is under more than one category.

USE OF THE INFORMATION

This form helps identify behavioral deficits and strengths and suggests to the therapist what behaviors might be targeted for observation and treatment. It also gives the therapist some information on the parents' perception of the child in many settings: the home, the school, the neighborhood, and the world at large. Ratings of 1s and 2s in the *Behavior Occurs* category and 4s and 5s in the *Need to Change* category should be compiled and prioritized within each category. The following questions should be considered when prioritizing:

1. Which behavior changes would be most beneficial for the child?
2. Which behavior changes would be most beneficial for the betterment of the parent-child relationship?
3. Which behavior changes are most easily achievable so that both parents and child receive positive reinforcement to keep working?
4. In terms of shaping, which behaviors are prerequisites for which other behaviors?

A readministration of the Behavior Status Checklist (P) after therapeutic intervention can serve as an indicator of therapeutic gains.

COMPARISON TO OTHER FORMS

BEHAVIOR STATUS CHECKLIST (C and A): In targeting behaviors for change it is often helpful to have the child or adolescent involved in the process. A compilation of similar items from the parents' and child or adolescent's forms will help establish target behaviors that suit both parents and youngster.

GUIDELINES FOR PARENTAL DISCIPLINE: By identifying the components of the behavioral repertoire of the child as they are viewed by the parents, the therapist can relate this information to the parents' style of discipline.

GUIDELINES FOR TIME-OUT: After identifying behaviors that parents view as maladaptive, the time-out procedure may be applied at the intervention stage.

PARENTAL REACTION SURVEY SCHEDULE: A parent who indicates that a great number of the child's behaviors need to be changed may also experience difficulty with effective discipline.

PROGRESS CHART: Once the target behaviors have been established, the Progress Chart can be useful in formulating treatment.

SCHOOL BEHAVIOR STATUS CHECKLIST: In some situations it may be important to find out if the problematic behaviors also are occurring in school.

SELF-EVALUATION SCALE: Use of this form in conjunction with the Behavior Status Checklist generally clarifies the problem areas.

RECOMMENDED READINGS

Refer to the Behavior Status Checklist (C and A), Recommended Readings Section.

BEHAVIOR STATUS CHECKLIST (P)

Parent filling out form _____ Date _____

Name of child _____ Date of birth _____

Circle the number in the first column that best describes how often your child performs the listed behavior and circle the number in the second column that indicates the degree to which you would like the frequency of the behavior to change.

1 — Not at all
2 — A little
3 — A fair amount
4 — Much
5 — Very much

	Behavior Occurs	*Need to Change*
1. Completes tasks or activities	1 2 3 4 5	1 2 3 4 5
2. Sits still for appropriate periods of time	1 2 3 4 5	1 2 3 4 5
3. Reads without prompting	1 2 3 4 5	1 2 3 4 5
4. Watches television	1 2 3 4 5	1 2 3 4 5
5. Participates in extracurricular school activities	1 2 3 4 5	1 2 3 4 5
6. Joins clubs	1 2 3 4 5	1 2 3 4 5
7. Joins sports	1 2 3 4 5	1 2 3 4 5
8. Performs well in school	1 2 3 4 5	1 2 3 4 5
9. Does what father tells him or her	1 2 3 4 5	1 2 3 4 5
10. Does what mother tells him or her	1 2 3 4 5	1 2 3 4 5
11. Does what teacher(s) tells him or her	1 2 3 4 5	1 2 3 4 5
12. Leaves home only with permission	1 2 3 4 5	1 2 3 4 5
13. Follows instructions	1 2 3 4 5	1 2 3 4 5
14. Pays attention when given instructions	1 2 3 4 5	1 2 3 4 5
15. Does what is told without displaying angry behavior	1 2 3 4 5	1 2 3 4 5
16. Eats what is served at mealtimes	1 2 3 4 5	1 2 3 4 5
17. Readily accepts no for an answer	1 2 3 4 5	1 2 3 4 5
18. Obeys father without talking back	1 2 3 4 5	1 2 3 4 5
19. Obeys mother without talking back	1 2 3 4 5	1 2 3 4 5
20. Obeys teacher(s) without talking back	1 2 3 4 5	1 2 3 4 5
21. Acts appropriately when taken shopping	1 2 3 4 5	1 2 3 4 5
22. Acts appropriately when taken out to eat	1 2 3 4 5	1 2 3 4 5
23. Has adequate eating and table manners	1 2 3 4 5	1 2 3 4 5
24. Attends school regularly	1 2 3 4 5	1 2 3 4 5
25. Does homework	1 2 3 4 5	1 2 3 4 5
26. Stays dry through the night	1 2 3 4 5	1 2 3 4 5
27. Stays dry through the day	1 2 3 4 5	1 2 3 4 5
28. Has control of bowel movements	1 2 3 4 5	1 2 3 4 5
29. Accepts failure well	1 2 3 4 5	1 2 3 4 5

	Behavior Occurs	Need to Change
30. Is clean and well-groomed	1 2 3 4 5	1 2 3 4 5
31. Refrains from complaining about physical symptoms	1 2 3 4 5	1 2 3 4 5
32. Makes age-appropriate decisions	1 2 3 4 5	1 2 3 4 5
33. Protects himself or herself from accidents and physical injury	1 2 3 4 5	1 2 3 4 5
34. Laughs at appropriate times	1 2 3 4 5	1 2 3 4 5
35. Exhibits age-appropriate behaviors	1 2 3 4 5	1 2 3 4 5
36. Exhibits gender-appropriate behaviors	1 2 3 4 5	1 2 3 4 5
37. Exhibits sexual behavior appropriate to age	1 2 3 4 5	1 2 3 4 5
38. Makes positive statements about himself or herself	1 2 3 4 5	1 2 3 4 5
39. Goes to sleep at night without difficulty	1 2 3 4 5	1 2 3 4 5
40. Sleeps through the night	1 2 3 4 5	1 2 3 4 5
41. Spends time alone	1 2 3 4 5	1 2 3 4 5
42. Handles new situations well	1 2 3 4 5	1 2 3 4 5
43. Eats appropriate amounts of food	1 2 3 4 5	1 2 3 4 5
44. Appears confident he or she will succeed	1 2 3 4 5	1 2 3 4 5
45. Feels comfortable about		
a. going to school	1 2 3 4 5	1 2 3 4 5
b. being around adult strangers	1 2 3 4 5	1 2 3 4 5
c. being around children who are strangers	1 2 3 4 5	1 2 3 4 5
d. being alone	1 2 3 4 5	1 2 3 4 5
e. being in new situations	1 2 3 4 5	1 2 3 4 5
46. Spends time with friends	1 2 3 4 5	1 2 3 4 5
47. Gets along well with peers	1 2 3 4 5	1 2 3 4 5
48. Kisses and hugs parents	1 2 3 4 5	1 2 3 4 5
49. Responds well to being kissed and hugged by parents	1 2 3 4 5	1 2 3 4 5
50. Responds well to criticism	1 2 3 4 5	1 2 3 4 5
51. Says nice things about others	1 2 3 4 5	1 2 3 4 5
52. Cooperates with others	1 2 3 4 5	1 2 3 4 5
53. Gets along well with adult neighbors	1 2 3 4 5	1 2 3 4 5
54. Gets along well with children in the neighborhood	1 2 3 4 5	1 2 3 4 5
55. Smiles	1 2 3 4 5	1 2 3 4 5
56. Plays solitary games	1 2 3 4 5	1 2 3 4 5
57. Plays games involving others	1 2 3 4 5	1 2 3 4 5
58. Has a good sense of humor	1 2 3 4 5	1 2 3 4 5
59. Is a good sport	1 2 3 4 5	1 2 3 4 5
60. Surprises you pleasantly	1 2 3 4 5	1 2 3 4 5
61. Shares with others	1 2 3 4 5	1 2 3 4 5
62. Gets along well with older brothers and sisters	1 2 3 4 5	1 2 3 4 5
63. Gets along well with younger brothers and sisters	1 2 3 4 5	1 2 3 4 5
64. Shares feelings and thoughts with mother	1 2 3 4 5	1 2 3 4 5
65. Shares feelings and thoughts with father	1 2 3 4 5	1 2 3 4 5

	Behavior Occurs	Need to Change
66. Plays with younger children	1 2 3 4 5	1 2 3 4 5
67. Handles competitive situations well	1 2 3 4 5	1 2 3 4 5
68. Respects the property of others	1 2 3 4 5	1 2 3 4 5
69. Tells the truth	1 2 3 4 5	1 2 3 4 5
70. Asks permission before using another person's possessions	1 2 3 4 5	1 2 3 4 5
71. Refrains from the use of violence	1 2 3 4 5	1 2 3 4 5

72. Please list any other behaviors of your child that you would like changed. Rate how often each behavior occurs and how much you feel it needs to be changed, using the same 5-point scale you used to rate the previous behaviors. _____

_____

_____

_____

_____

_____

_____

ADDENDUM FOR ADOLESCENTS

	Behavior Occurs	Need to Change
73. Makes friends easily	1 2 3 4 5	1 2 3 4 5
74. Has consistent moods	1 2 3 4 5	1 2 3 4 5
75. Appears relaxed in social situations	1 2 3 4 5	1 2 3 4 5
76. If employed, is considered reliable on the job	1 2 3 4 5	1 2 3 4 5
77. Shows up on time for		
a. work	1 2 3 4 5	1 2 3 4 5
b. school	1 2 3 4 5	1 2 3 4 5
c. family meals and activities	1 2 3 4 5	1 2 3 4 5
d. curfew	1 2 3 4 5	1 2 3 4 5
e. other responsibilities	1 2 3 4 5	1 2 3 4 5
78. Does assigned chores	1 2 3 4 5	1 2 3 4 5
79. Refrains from the use of marijuana	1 2 3 4 5	1 2 3 4 5
80. Refrains from the use of hard drugs such as heroin or amphetamines	1 2 3 4 5	1 2 3 4 5
81. Refrains from the use of alcohol	1 2 3 4 5	1 2 3 4 5
82. Refrains from the use of cigarettes	1 2 3 4 5	1 2 3 4 5
83. Refrains from what you would call excessive swearing	1 2 3 4 5	1 2 3 4 5
84. Refrains from the use of obscene language	1 2 3 4 5	1 2 3 4 5
85. Has friends you approve of	1 2 3 4 5	1 2 3 4 5
86. Has your approval on the degree of emotional involvement with the opposite sex	1 2 3 4 5	1 2 3 4 5
87. Has your approval on the degree of physical involvement with the opposite sex	1 2 3 4 5	1 2 3 4 5
88. Keeps his or her room clean	1 2 3 4 5	1 2 3 4 5

BEHAVIOR STATUS CHECKLIST (C and A)

RATIONALE/PURPOSE

Involving the child or adolescent in the identification and treatment of his problems often is an enlightening and helpful approach. Parents may not be aware of some of the behavioral deficits or excesses that are affecting the youngster. The child's or adolescent's perception of the appropriateness of a given behavior and its frequency, intensity, and duration may differ markedly from the parents' perception of these same components.

The Behavior Status Checklist (C and A) has been designed to aid in the identification of adaptive and maladaptive behaviors and to involve the youngster in the decision-making process of choosing behaviors to be targeted for change. Items are stated in the positive so that the youngster notes his positive behaviors as well as his negative ones. The adolescent form has a 5-point scale for each category, while the children's form has only a 3-point scale.

ADMINISTRATION

The therapist should oversee the administration and use of this form. It is to be filled out by the child or adolescent. Small children may need assistance in reading the items and choosing the appropriate categories.

GUIDELINES

1. This form is part of the Intake Packet. It is administered to the youngster during the first or second session, with the therapist helping to answer questions and give explanations where necessary.
2. The *Need to Change* category should be answered in terms of what the child himself would like to change and not in terms of what the child thinks others would like to see changed.

ITEM BREAKDOWN

FORM C

Number of questions: 58

Questions	Topic
1–4, 13	Attentional behaviors
5–8	School and extracurricular activities
9–12, 14–19, 20*, 21*, 24	Compliance behaviors
20*, 21*, 22, 23, 25, 26, 28, 29*, 54–57	Responsibility/self-control behaviors
30	Age-appropriate behaviors
27, 31–35, 43*	Adaptive/relaxed functioning
29*, 36–43*, 44–53	Social behaviors
58	Other behaviors

FORM A

Number of questions: 106

Questions	Topic
1–4, 14	Attentional behaviors
5–8	School and extracurricular activities
9–13, 15–20, 21*, 22*, 25	Compliance behaviors
21*, 22*, 23, 24, 26–28, 30, 31, 33 34*, 50, 68–71, 75–84, 87	Responsibility/self-control behaviors
32, 35–37	Age- and sex-appropriate behaviors
29, 38–45, 55*, 58, 73, 74*	Adaptive/relaxed functioning
34*, 46–49, 51–56*, 57, 59–67, 72, 74*	Social behaviors
85, 86	Sexual behaviors
88–106	Overt/covert behaviors in need of change
107	Other behaviors

*This indicates that the item is under more than one category.

USE OF THE INFORMATION

This form aids in the identification of behavioral deficits and strengths and suggests to the therapist what behaviors might be targeted for observation and treatment. It gives the therapist information on the child's perception of himself.

In the children's form the *Behavior Occurs* items that should be compiled and prioritized within that category are the ones under *Not at all* and *Sometimes,* and the *Need to Change* items to work with are those under *Yes.* In the adolescents' form the ratings of 1s and 2s in the *Behavior Occurs* category and the 4s and 5s in the *Need to Change* category should be compiled and prioritized within each category. Prioritizing should be done with consideration of the following points:

1. Which behavior changes would be most beneficial for the child?
2. Which behavior changes would be most beneficial for the betterment of the parent-child relationship?
3. Which behavior changes are most easily achievable so that both parents and child receive positive reinforcement to keep working?
4. In terms of shaping, which behaviors are prerequisites for which other behaviors?
5. Which items match up with items on the Behavior Status Checklist (P)?
6. Which behaviors does the child or adolescent want most to see changed?

COMPARISON TO OTHER FORMS

BEHAVIOR RECORD FORM: The Behavior Status Checklists suggest to the therapist which behaviors warrant observation; the Behavior Record Form provides a form on which to record these observations.

BEHAVIOR STATUS CHECKLIST (P): A comparison of this checklist with the child's or adolescent's Behavior Status Checklist should reveal problematic behaviors in the home and perhaps elsewhere. The comparison also may indicate to the therapist areas in which the perceptions of difficulty differ between parent and child.

BEHAVIORAL RATING CARD: Using the Behavior Status Checklist (C and A) to identify behaviors a child wishes to change can be a means of involving the child in an intervention program using the Behavioral Rating Card.

FEAR INVENTORY: A client who indicates several behaviors in need of change or improvement may indicate that exaggerated fears are among those behaviors.

HOME VISIT OBSERVATION FORM: The Behavior Status Checklists will give the home observer an idea of which problematic behaviors should be measured.

PROGRESS CHART: The Behavior Status Checklist (C and A) may be helpful in determining which behaviors are most appropriate to target.

RESPONSE COST SURVEY SCHEDULE: Once the behaviors to be targeted for change have been identified by the Behavior Status Checklists, the items on the Response Cost Survey Schedule may be of assistance in providing consequences for certain behaviors.

SCHOOL BEHAVIOR STATUS CHECKLIST: By using the Behavior Status Checklist (C and A) in conjunction with this checklist, the therapist will probably develop some understanding of what behaviors may need to be changed in the school environment.

SELF-EVALUATION SCALE: Often the Behavior Status Checklist (C and A) gives some indication that the youngster does not perceive himself in a very positive light. The therapist may want to find out more about the client's self-appraisal and the Self-Evaluation Scale can be quite useful for this.

SESSION REPORT: The Session Report should be made with reference to the Behavior Status Checklist so a comparison can be made between weekly interventions and presenting complaints.

RECOMMENDED READINGS

Bellack, A. S., & Hersen, M. *Behavior modification: An introductory textbook.* Baltimore: Williams and Wilkins, 1977. (a)

Bellack, A. S., & Hersen, M. The use of self-report inventories in behavioral assessment. In J. D. Cone & R. P. Hawkins (Eds.), *Behavioral assessment: New directions in clinical psychology.* New York: Brunner/Mazel, 1977. (b)

Eisler, R. M. The behavioral assessment of social skills. In M. Hersen & A. S. Bellack (Eds.), *Behavioral assessment: A practical handbook.* Elmsford, N.Y.: Pergamon Press, 1976.

Wahl, G., Johnson, S. M., Johansson, S., & Martin, S. An operant analysis of child-family interaction. *Behavior Therapy,* 1974, *5,* 64–78.

Wahler, R. G. Deviant child behavior within the family. In H. Leitenberg (Ed.), *Handbook of behavior modification and behavior therapy.* Englewood Cliffs, N.J.: Prentice-Hall, 1976.

BEHAVIOR STATUS CHECKLIST (C)

Name _____ Date _____

Age _____ Sex: Boy _____ Girl _____

School _____ Grade _____

Here are some things that children do. Which ones do you do? Put an X in the box that tells best how much you do each behavior. These are your choices for answers:

Not at all. I never do that.

Sometimes I do that.

Most of the time I do that.

Which behaviors would you like to change? Put an X in the box that tells whether or not you want to change how often you do that behavior. You can choose one of two answers:

Yes, I want to change how often I do that.

No, I don't want to change how often I do that.

	Behavior Occurs			Need to Change	
	Not at all	Sometimes	Most of the time	Yes	No
1. I finish what I start.					
2. I sit still.					
3. I read books without being told to.					
4. I watch television.					
5. I join clubs at school.					
6. I join clubs outside of school (Cub Scouts, Brownies).					
7. I join sports.					
8. I work hard in school.					
9. I do what my father tells me.					
10. I do what my mother tells me.					
11. I do what my teacher tells me.					
12. I ask for permission before leaving home.					
13. I listen when someone tells me how to do something.					
14. I do what I am told without crying.					
15. I eat what is on my plate.					
16. I take no for an answer without crying or getting upset.					
17. I do what my father tells me without talking back.					
18. I do what my mother tells me without talking back.					
19. I do what my teacher tells me without talking back.					

	Behavior Occurs			Need to Change	
	Not at all	Sometimes	Most of the time	Yes	No
20. I am good when I am out shopping with someone.					
21. I am good when I go out to eat with someone.					
22. I eat my food without making a mess.					
23. I go to school when I am supposed to.					
24. I do my homework.					
25. I have dry pants when I wake up in the morning.					
26. I have dry pants during the day.					
27. I lose at sports or games without crying or getting mad.					
28. I keep myself clean.					
29. I laugh when things are funny.					
30. I act like other kids my age.					
31. I think nice things about myself.					
32. I go to sleep at night soon after I go to bed.					
33. I sleep through the night without waking up.					
34. I spend time alone.					
35. I like					
a. going to school.					
b. being around adults I don't know.					
c. being around kids I don't know.					
d. being by myself.					
e. going to new places.					
36. I spend time with friends.					
37. I get along well with kids my age.					
38. I kiss and hug my parents.					
39. I like my parents to kiss and hug me.					
40. I say nice things about other people.					
41. I get along with kids in the neighborhood.					
42. I smile.					
43. I play games by myself.					
44. I play games with other kids.					
45. I am a good sport.					
46. I do nice things for my parents.					

	Behavior Occurs			Need to Change	
	Not at all	Sometimes	Most of the time	Yes	No
47. I share with others.					
48. I get along well with my brothers and sisters.					
49. I tell my mother about things that make me sad.					
50. I tell my mother about things that are important to me.					
51. I tell my father about things that make me sad.					
52. I tell my father about things that are important to me.					
53. I play with younger children.					
54. I take good care of things that belong to others.					
55. I take good care of things that belong to me.					
56. I tell the truth.					
57. I ask permission before using something that belongs to someone else.					

58. Please write down any other behaviors you would like to change. Tell if they happen *Not at all,* *Sometimes,* or *Most of the time.*

_____

_____

_____

_____

_____

_____

BEHAVIOR STATUS CHECKLIST (A)

Name _____ Date _____

Age _____ Sex _____

School (if in school) _____ Grade _____

Occupation (if employed) _____

Circle the number in the first column that best describes how often you perform the listed behavior and circle the number in the second column that indicates the degree to which you would like the frequency of the behavior to change.

1 — Not at all
2 — A little
3 — A fair amount
4 — Much
5 — Very much

	Behavior Occurs	Need to Change
1. Complete tasks or activities	1 2 3 4 5	1 2 3 4 5
2. Sit still for appropriate periods of time	1 2 3 4 5	1 2 3 4 5
3. Read without being prompted	1 2 3 4 5	1 2 3 4 5
4. Watch television	1 2 3 4 5	1 2 3 4 5
5. Participate in extracurricular school activities	1 2 3 4 5	1 2 3 4 5
6. Join clubs	1 2 3 4 5	1 2 3 4 5
7. Join sports	1 2 3 4 5	1 2 3 4 5
8. Perform well in school	1 2 3 4 5	1 2 3 4 5
9. Do what your father tells you	1 2 3 4 5	1 2 3 4 5
10. Do what your mother tells you	1 2 3 4 5	1 2 3 4 5
11. Do what your teacher(s) tells you	1 2 3 4 5	1 2 3 4 5
12. Leave home only with permission	1 2 3 4 5	1 2 3 4 5
13. Follow instructions	1 2 3 4 5	1 2 3 4 5
14. Pay attention when given instructions	1 2 3 4 5	1 2 3 4 5
15. Do what you are told without displaying angry behavior	1 2 3 4 5	1 2 3 4 5
16. Eat what is served at mealtimes	1 2 3 4 5	1 2 3 4 5
17. Readily accept no for an answer	1 2 3 4 5	1 2 3 4 5
18. Obey your father without talking back	1 2 3 4 5	1 2 3 4 5
19. Obey your mother without talking back	1 2 3 4 5	1 2 3 4 5
20. Obey your teacher(s) without talking back	1 2 3 4 5	1 2 3 4 5
21. Act appropriately when taken shopping	1 2 3 4 5	1 2 3 4 5
22. Act appropriately when taken out to eat	1 2 3 4 5	1 2 3 4 5
23. Have adequate eating and table manners	1 2 3 4 5	1 2 3 4 5
24. Attend school regularly	1 2 3 4 5	1 2 3 4 5
25. Do your homework	1 2 3 4 5	1 2 3 4 5
26. Stay dry through the night	1 2 3 4 5	1 2 3 4 5
27. Stay dry through the day	1 2 3 4 5	1 2 3 4 5

	Behavior Occurs	Need to Change
28. Have control of bowel movements	1 2 3 4 5	1 2 3 4 5
29. Accept failure well	1 2 3 4 5	1 2 3 4 5
30. Are clean and well-groomed	1 2 3 4 5	1 2 3 4 5
31. Refrain from complaining about physical symptoms	1 2 3 4 5	1 2 3 4 5
32. Make decisions appropriate for your age	1 2 3 4 5	1 2 3 4 5
33. Protect yourself from accidents and physical injury	1 2 3 4 5	1 2 3 4 5
34. Laugh at the right times	1 2 3 4 5	1 2 3 4 5
35. Exhibit behaviors that are appropriate for your age	1 2 3 4 5	1 2 3 4 5
36. Exhibit behaviors toward the opposite sex that are appropriate for your age	1 2 3 4 5	1 2 3 4 5
37. Exhibit behaviors that are appropriate for your gender (male/female)	1 2 3 4 5	1 2 3 4 5
38. Make positive statements about yourself	1 2 3 4 5	1 2 3 4 5
39. Go to sleep at night without difficulty	1 2 3 4 5	1 2 3 4 5
40. Sleep through the night	1 2 3 4 5	1 2 3 4 5
41. Spend time alone	1 2 3 4 5	1 2 3 4 5
42. Handle new situations well	1 2 3 4 5	1 2 3 4 5
43. Eat appropriate amounts of food	1 2 3 4 5	1 2 3 4 5
44. Feel confident you will succeed	1 2 3 4 5	1 2 3 4 5
45. Feel comfortable about		
a. going to school	1 2 3 4 5	1 2 3 4 5
b. being around adult strangers	1 2 3 4 5	1 2 3 4 5
c. being around people your own age who are strangers	1 2 3 4 5	1 2 3 4 5
d. being alone	1 2 3 4 5	1 2 3 4 5
e. being in new situations	1 2 3 4 5	1 2 3 4 5
46. Spend time with your friends	1 2 3 4 5	1 2 3 4 5
47. Get along well with people your own age	1 2 3 4 5	1 2 3 4 5
48. Kiss and hug your parents	1 2 3 4 5	1 2 3 4 5
49. Like being kissed and hugged by your parents	1 2 3 4 5	1 2 3 4 5
50. Respond well to criticism	1 2 3 4 5	1 2 3 4 5
51. Say nice things about others	1 2 3 4 5	1 2 3 4 5
52. Cooperate with others	1 2 3 4 5	1 2 3 4 5
53. Get along well with adult neighbors	1 2 3 4 5	1 2 3 4 5
54. Get along well with people your age in the neighborhood	1 2 3 4 5	1 2 3 4 5
55. Smile	1 2 3 4 5	1 2 3 4 5
56. Play solitary games	1 2 3 4 5	1 2 3 4 5
57. Play games involving others	1 2 3 4 5	1 2 3 4 5
58. Have a good sense of humor	1 2 3 4 5	1 2 3 4 5
59. Are a good sport	1 2 3 4 5	1 2 3 4 5
60. Surprise your parents pleasantly	1 2 3 4 5	1 2 3 4 5
61. Share with others	1 2 3 4 5	1 2 3 4 5
62. Get along well with older brothers and sisters	1 2 3 4 5	1 2 3 4 5

	Behavior Occurs	Need to Change
63. Get along well with younger brothers and sisters	1 2 3 4 5	1 2 3 4 5
64. Share your feelings and thoughts with your mother	1 2 3 4 5	1 2 3 4 5
65. Share your feelings and thoughts with your father	1 2 3 4 5	1 2 3 4 5
66. Spend time with younger children	1 2 3 4 5	1 2 3 4 5
67. Handle competitive situations well	1 2 3 4 5	1 2 3 4 5
68. Respect the property of others	1 2 3 4 5	1 2 3 4 5
69. Tell the truth	1 2 3 4 5	1 2 3 4 5
70. Ask permission before using another person's possessions	1 2 3 4 5	1 2 3 4 5
71. Refrain from the use of violence	1 2 3 4 5	1 2 3 4 5
72. Make friends easily	1 2 3 4 5	1 2 3 4 5
73. Have consistent moods	1 2 3 4 5	1 2 3 4 5
74. Are relaxed in social situations	1 2 3 4 5	1 2 3 4 5
75. Are considered reliable on the job	1 2 3 4 5	1 2 3 4 5
76. Show up on time for		
a. work	1 2 3 4 5	1 2 3 4 5
b. school	1 2 3 4 5	1 2 3 4 5
c. family meals and activities	1 2 3 4 5	1 2 3 4 5
d. curfew	1 2 3 4 5	1 2 3 4 5
e. other responsibilities	1 2 3 4 5	1 2 3 4 5
77. Do your chores	1 2 3 4 5	1 2 3 4 5
78. Refrain from the use of marijuana	1 2 3 4 5	1 2 3 4 5
79. Refrain from the use of hard drugs such as heroin or amphetamines	1 2 3 4 5	1 2 3 4 5
80. Refrain from the use of alcohol	1 2 3 4 5	1 2 3 4 5
81. Refrain from the use of cigarettes	1 2 3 4 5	1 2 3 4 5
82. Refrain from excessive swearing	1 2 3 4 5	1 2 3 4 5
83. Refrain from the use of obscene language	1 2 3 4 5	1 2 3 4 5
84. Have friends your parents approve of	1 2 3 4 5	1 2 3 4 5
85. Have the approval of your parents on the degree of emotional involvement with the opposite sex	1 2 3 4 5	1 2 3 4 5
86. Have the approval of your parents on the degree of physical involvement with the opposite sex	1 2 3 4 5	1 2 3 4 5
87. Keep your room clean	1 2 3 4 5	1 2 3 4 5

Check the following skills you would like to learn:

88. _____ To overcome a feeling of nausea when you are nervous

89. _____ To stop thinking about things that depress you

90. _____ To stop thinking about things that make you anxious

91. _____ To feel less anxious in crowds

92. _____ To stop worrying about your physical condition

93. _____ To stop biting your fingernails

94. _____ To feel less anxious about being alone

95. _____ To stop thinking the same thoughts over and over

96. _____ To stop thinking people are against you or out to get you

97. _____ To stop having headaches

98. _____ To stop daydreaming a lot

99. _____ To control a desire to yell at or hit other people when you are angry

100. _____ To stop bothering people too much

101. _____ To be less forgetful

102. _____ To stop thinking about committing suicide

103. _____ To stop putting off things that need to be done

104. _____ To stop thinking about things that make you feel guilty

105. _____ To talk to people

106. _____ To not be upset when others criticize you

107. Please describe any other skills you would like to learn.

_____

_____

_____

_____

REINFORCEMENT SURVEY SCHEDULES (C and A)

Children's Reinforcement Survey Schedules*
Adolescents' Reinforcement Survey Schedule

RATIONALE/PURPOSE

The Children's Reinforcement Survey Schedules (by Cautela and Brion-Meisels) and the Adolescents' Reinforcement Survey Schedule (by Cautela and LaCross) were developed for the identification of positive stimuli that can be used to shape and maintain desirable behaviors.

The Children's Reinforcement Survey Schedules consist of three schedules. The first two (A and B) were constructed for use with children in kindergarten through third grade, and each contains 25 items. The student is asked to rate her preference for each item according to a 3-point scale with the choices of *Dislike, Like,* or *Like very much.* This 3-point scale was chosen to simplify the attentional demands on children, since a 5-point scale (such as that used on the Adolescents' Reinforcement Survey Schedule) requires more sophisticated relational judgments. The first two schedules (A and B) both include the same general categories, although different items are used in each. Individual items were chosen for their age-appropriateness and usefulness as overt as well as covert reinforcers. One schedule may be used for the initial identification of reinforcers, while the other may be used for further exploration. Schedule C, for fourth through sixth graders, contains a total of 80 items. The first 75 items ask children to rate their preferences on the same 3-point scale used in Schedules A and B. The categories include all those found in Schedules A and B except for toys plus a problem-solving category. Five open-ended questions are included at the end of this schedule.

The Adolescents' Reinforcement Survey Schedule consists of 90 items constructed on a 5-point scale from *Not at all* to *Very much.* Most of the items on this schedule have to do with relations with other people, since this is usually a period of life in which the adolescent broadens out in social relations from the nuclear family to peers and other significant adults.

ADMINISTRATION

The Children's Reinforcement Survey Schedules can be administered individually or in groups. Although all three schedules have written directions, an explanation of the purpose and procedure should be given orally by the administrator. It is suggested that the person administering the scales be a therapist, counselor, or someone other than the parent or teacher, since some items on the scales relate to reinforcement from interactions with parents and teachers. It is further suggested that children in grades K through 3 be read the items orally and guided in filling out the appropriate spaces. Those children in grades 4 through 6 with sufficient reading skills can work independently on the written form.

The Adolescents' Reinforcement Survey Schedule can also be administered individually or in groups with clients working independently. This too should be administered by a therapist, counselor, or paraprofessional, and, when completed, should be brought to the next counseling session.

GUIDELINES

1. During the oral administration of Schedules A or B to children in grades K through 3, the administrator should frequently repeat the 3-point scale after reading each item.

---

*Reprinted with permission of publisher from: Cautela, J. R., & Brion-Meisels, L. A children's reinforcement survey schedule. PSYCHOLOGICAL REPORTS, 1979, *44,* 327–338, Table 1.

The Adolescents' Reinforcement Survey Schedule was developed in collaboration with Suzanne LaCross.

2. When administering the Children's Reinforcement Survey Schedules to very young children in groups, the number in the group should be no larger than four. The time spent in attending to group members for any group larger than this would negate the time-saving benefits of group administration.

3. Older children (grades 4–6) who have been identified as having problems with reading or attention span may need oral administration or repetition by the administrator of the 3-point rating scale.

4. Schedules A and B of the Children's Reinforcement Survey Schedules usually each take about 20 minutes to administer. Schedule C usually takes about 35 minutes.

5. Adolescent clients can usually complete the Adolescents' Reinforcement Survey Schedule in about 30 minutes.

6. It may well be possible to use an appropriate schedule from the Children's Reinforcement Survey Schedules with children younger than kindergarten age. It is advised, however, that it be administered orally, on a one-to-one basis, and that the administrator be reasonably certain that the child understands the instructions as well as each item.

ITEM BREAKDOWN

CHILDREN'S REINFORCEMENT SURVEY SCHEDULES
SCHEDULES A AND B

Number of questions: 25 each

A Questions	B Questions	Topic
1–3	1–3	Food
4	4	Toys
5, 6	5, 6	Crafts
7	7	Music
8, 13	8	Reading
9, 10	9, 10	Sports
11, 12, 15	11, 13, 15, 16	School
14, 16, 24	12, 14, 25	Self-esteem
17–20	17–19	Other leisure activities
21, 25	20, 21	Animals
22, 23	22–24	Relationships with people

SCHEDULE C

Number of questions: 80

Questions	Topic
1–3	Food
4–10	Crafts
11–13	Problem solving
14–26	Sports
27–29	Music
30–34	Reading
35–41	Other leisure activities
42–50	School
51–54	Animals
55–63	Relationships with people
64–75	Self-esteem
76	Best characteristic

Questions	Topic
77	Daydreams
78	Fun activities
79	Birthday presents
80	Collections

ADOLESCENTS' REINFORCEMENT SURVEY SCHEDULE

Number of questions: 90

Questions	Topic
1–12	Family members and the home
13–27	Friends
28–34	Preferred age groups
35–47	School and school-related activities
48–64	Members of the opposite sex
65–81	Free-time activities
82, 83	Appearance
84–89	Eating, drinking, smoking, and taking drugs
90	Other experiences

USE OF THE INFORMATION

The Reinforcement Survey Schedules can be used in three general ways: initially in the behavioral assessment, later in clinical procedures applicable either in individual or group settings, and in research.

By definition, a positive reinforcer is a stimulus that increases the rate of the response it follows. Therefore, the final labeling of any item as a reinforcer can only be done after observing the effect of the item on the behavior of the youngster. The therapist should identify possible reinforcers through the client's verbal or written report (as on these forms), through observations of the youngster as she interacts with the environment, and through information obtained from significant others; only then should he decide to actually use the highly rated item to increase behavior.

The appearance of *many* low-rated items on a client's form may suggest depression (lack of reinforcement in the environment), fear, and/or withdrawal on the part of the youngster. On the Adolescents' Reinforcement Survey Schedule, it is suggested that the administrator be alert for the adolescent who doesn't rate items on interactions with peers as very reinforcing. Low ratings on such items may point to faulty patterns in learning to seek reinforcement outside the family, as is appropriate for members of this age group. Of course, if any one area is consistently rated low, e.g., all interactions with family members, it should lead the therapist to explore this area and perhaps target it for intervention.

Highly rated items from the Schedules may be used as immediate overt or covert reinforcers or as back-up overt reinforcers for token procedures. The information received from these schedules is easily applicable in a wide range of situations from the youngster's daily life, e.g., the classroom, out-of-school programs, or traditional clinical settings.

The administration of these scales also helps in establishing rapport with a client. It is possible to make available during the therapeutic hour specific activities that are reinforcing to the client, contingent upon her paying attention and practicing the techniques being taught.

For research purposes, following successful reliability assessment with a specific clinical population, the results obtained could be compared with treatment outcomes.

The Reinforcement Survey Schedules are valuable tools for quickly determining probable reinforcing consequences which can be used both to increase deficit behaviors and decrease inappropriate ones in children and adolescents. The ease of administration of the Schedules makes them especially valuable to a variety of professionals working in different settings with these age groups.

COMPARISON TO OTHER FORMS

BEHAVIORAL RATING CARD: Reinforcements for a successful program using the Behavioral Rating Card may be taken directly from the Reinforcement Survey Schedules.

FEAR INVENTORY: A client with a high number of reported fears will often express a low number of reinforcers enjoyed in her environment. Items on the Reinforcement Survey Schedules can be used to reinforce anti-anxiety behaviors.

GUIDELINES FOR PARENTAL DISCIPLINE: Parents may find the Reinforcement Survey Schedules helpful in establishing positive consequences in their discipline program.

MOTIVATION ASSESSMENT OF PARENTS AND CHILDREN: If motivation is assessed as being low, a review of the Reinforcement Survey Schedules would be helpful. Perhaps the rewards being used for behavior change are not in fact reinforcements at the present time.

PARENTS' AND CHILDREN'S REINFORCEMENT SURVEY SCHEDULE: Many items on this scale correlate with items on the Reinforcement Survey Schedules and as such provide a good reliability measure.

PROGRESS CHART: Rewards necessary to the success of the program set up on the Progress Chart can be taken from information supplied on the Reinforcement Survey Schedules.

REINFORCEMENT MENU: Highly rated items may be taken from the Reinforcement Survey Schedules to contribute to the designing of a Reinforcement Menu for the client (reinforcements immediately available at any time).

SCHOOL REINFORCEMENT SURVEY SCHEDULE: Several items on this scale are also related to items on the Reinforcement Survey Schedules. Correlations should be noted.

SELF-EVALUATION SCALE: A poor self-image is often reported by clients who experience a lack of reinforcement in their environment.

SESSION REPORT: It is important to continuously reassess the reinforcements being applied both in and outside of therapy in the Session Report.

RECOMMENDED READINGS

Bersoff, D. N., & Moyer, D. Positive reinforcement observation schedule (PROS): Development and use. In E. J. Mash & L. G. Terdal (Eds.), *Behavior therapy assessment: Diagnosis, design and evaluation.* New York: Springer, 1976.

Cautela, J. R., & Brion-Meisels, L. A children's reinforcement survey schedule. *Psychological Reports,* 1979, *44,* 327–338.

Clement, P. W., & Richard, R. C. Identifying reinforcers for children: A children's reinforcement survey. In E. J. Mash & L. G. Terdal (Eds.), *Behavior therapy assessment: Diagnosis, design and evaluation.* New York: Springer, 1976.

Ferster, C. B., & Skinner, B. F. *Schedules of reinforcement.* New York: Appleton-Century-Crofts, 1957.

Firestone, P., & Douglas, V. I. The effects of verbal and material rewards and punishers on the performance of impulsive and reflective children. *Child Study Journal,* 1975, *7,* 71–78.

CHILDREN'S REINFORCEMENT SURVEY SCHEDULES (C)

Schedule A*

Name _____ Date _____

Age _____ Sex: Boy _____ Girl _____

School _____ Grade _____

This is a list of many different things or activities. Explain how much you like each choice by making an X in the appropriate box.

If you dislike the choice, make an X in the box under Dislike:

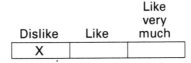

If you like the choice, make an X in the box under Like:

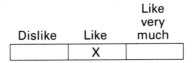

If the choice is something that you like very, very much, make an X in the box under Like very much:

	Dislike	Like	Like very much
1. Do you like candy?			
2. Do you like raisins?			
3. Do you like milk?			
4. Do you like stuffed toy animals?			
5. Do you like coloring?			
6. Do you like making things out of clay?			
7. Do you like listening to music?			
8. Do you like animal stories?			
9. Do you like playing on swings?			
10. Do you like kickball?			
11. Do you like going on field trips at school?			
12. Do you like being the teacher's helper?			
13. Do you like going to the library?			
14. Do you like people to tell you that you did a good job?			
15. Do you like your teacher to buy materials that you especially like?			
16. Do you like teaching things to other people?			

*Reproduced with permission of publisher by an offset process from: Cautela, J. R., & Brion-Meisels, L. A children's reinforcement survey schedule. PSYCHOLOGICAL REPORTS, 1979, *44,* 327–338, Table 1.

	Dislike	Like	Like very much
17. Do you like watching trucks, bulldozers, and tractors?			
18. Do you like to go shopping?			
19. Do you like to eat out in a restaurant?			
20. Do you like going to a circus or a fair?			
21. Do you like playing with dogs?			
22. Do you like to play with some children younger than you?			
23. Do you like to play with some special grown-ups?			
24. Do you like people to take care of you when you are sick?			
25. Do you like taking care of pet animals?			

CHILDREN'S REINFORCEMENT SURVEY SCHEDULES (C)

Schedule B

Name _____ Date _____

Age _____ Sex: Boy _____ Girl _____

School _____ Grade _____

This is a list of many different things or activities. Explain how much you like each choice by making an X in the appropriate box.

If you dislike the choice, make an X in the box under Dislike:

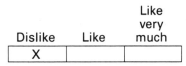

If you like the choice, make an X in the box under Like:

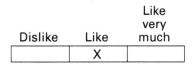

If the choice is something that you like very, very much, make an X in the box under Like very much:

	Dislike	Like	Like very much
			X

	Dislike	Like	Like very much
1. Do you like apples?			
2. Do you like breakfast cereals?			
3. Do you like fruit juice?			
4. Do you like to play with toy cars?			
5. Do you like painting?			
6. Do you like making things out of wood?			
7. Do you like to sing?			
8. Do you like cartoons and comic books?			
9. Do you like swimming?			
10. Do you like riding a bike?			
11. Do you like outdoor recess?			
12. Do you like to be the winner of a contest?			
13. Do you like arithmetic and working with numbers?			
14. Do you like being better than everyone else at something?			
15. Do you like saving your school papers to show to other people?			
16. Do you like your parents to ask you what you did in school today?			
17. Do you like to watch TV?			
18. Do you like traveling to different, far-away places on vacation?			

	Dislike	Like	Like very much
19. Do you like to go to the movies?			
20. Do you like playing with cats?			
21. Do you like to go to the zoo?			
22. Do you like playing with some children older than you?			
23. Do you like being alone rather than being with other people?			
24. If your friend is sick, do you like to take some things to your friend's house to make your friend feel happier?			
25. Do you like someone to take care of you when you are scared?			

CHILDREN'S REINFORCEMENT SURVEY SCHEDULES (C)

Schedule C

Name _____ Date _____

Age _____ Sex: Boy _____ Girl _____

School _____ Grade _____

This is a list of many different things or activities. Explain how much you like each choice by making an X in the appropriate box.

If you dislike the choice, make an X in the box under Dislike:

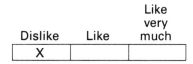

If you like the choice, make an X in the box under Like:

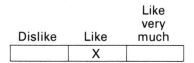

If the choice is something that you like very, very much, make an X in the box under Like very much:

	Dislike	Like	Like very much
			X

	Dislike	Like	Like very much
1. Do you like candy?			
2. Do you like fruit?			
3. Do you like soda?			
4. Do you like cooking?			
5. Do you like to make models?			
6. Do you like to play with model cars and trains?			
7. Do you like to draw and paint?			
8. Do you like to do crafts?			
9. Do you like carpentry and woodworking?			
10. Do you like making things out of clay?			
11. Do you like working with motors?			
12. Do you like puzzles?			
13. Do you like fixing broken things?			
14. Would you like to have sports equipment of your own?			
15. Do you like to play on playground equipment?			
16. Do you like to go bike riding?			
17. Do you like to go swimming?			
18. Do you like to go skiing?			

	Dislike	Like	Like very much
19. Do you like hockey?			
20. Do you like baseball?			
21. Do you like football?			
22. Do you like basketball?			
23. Do you like kickball?			
24. Do you like camping?			
25. Do you like go-carts?			
26. Do you like mini-bikes?			
27. Do you like listening to music?			
28. Do you like singing?			
29. Do you like learning how to play musical instruments?			
30. Do you like cartoons and comic books?			
31. Do you like fairy tales?			
32. Do you like science fiction?			
33. Do you like mysteries?			
34. Do you like biographies (stories about people's lives)?			
35. Do you like to sell things?			
36. Do you like to go shopping?			
37. Do you like to watch TV?			
38. Do you like to go to different, far-away places on vacation?			
39. Do you like to eat out in a restaurant?			
40. Do you like to go to the movies?			
41. Would you like to go to a circus or a fair?			
42. Do you like going on field trips at school?			
43. Do you like outdoor recess?			
44. Do you like it when your teacher buys materials that you especially like?			
45. Do you like being a leader in your class, such as being a class officer?			
46. Do you like giving reports in front of the class?			
47. Do you like creative writing (making up stories or poems)?			
48. Do you like science?			
49. Do you like math?			
50. Do you like spelling?			
51. Do you like playing with dogs?			
52. Do you like playing with cats?			
53. Do you like to go to the zoo?			
54. Do you like taking care of pet animals?			
55. Do you like to play with some children younger than you?			
56. Do you like to play with some children older than you?			
57. Do you like to play with some special grownups?			
58. Do you like being alone rather than being with other people?			

	Dislike	Like	Like very much
59. Would you like to talk to a sports star you know about?			
60. Would you like to talk to a TV or movie star you have seen?			
61. Do you like going to parties?			
62. Do you like to stay overnight at a friend's house?			
63. If your friend is sick, do you like to take some things to your friend's house to make your friend feel happier?			
64. Do you like earning money?			
65. Do you like to be praised for your good work?			
66. Do you like your parents to ask you what you did in school today?			
67. Do you like to be the winner of a contest?			
68. Do you like to have your teacher ask you to help?			
69. Do you like getting the right answer?			
70. Do you like to show your good work to other people?			
71. Do you feel good when you have just finished a project or job you had to do?			
72. Do you like it when all the other kids think you are terrific?			
73. Do you like having a birthday party and getting presents?			
74. Do you like someone to take care of you when you are scared?			
75. If you are sick, do you like people to take care of you?			

76. What do you think is the best thing about you? _____

_____

_____

_____

77. What do you daydream about? _____

_____

_____

_____

78. What do you do for fun? _____

_____

_____

_____

79. What would you like for your birthday? _____

_____

_____

_____

80. Do you have any collections? _____ If so, what do you collect? _____

_____

_____

_____

ADOLESCENTS' REINFORCEMENT SURVEY SCHEDULE (A)

Name _____ Date _____

Age _____ Sex _____

School (if in school) _____ Grade _____

Occupation (if employed) _____

Put a check mark in the column that best describes how much you like each of the following experiences.

	Not at all	A little	A fair amount	Much	Very much
1. Talking with your brother and/or sister					
2. Going out to eat with your brother and/or sister					
3. Going places with your brother and/or sister					
4. Telling secrets to your brother and/or sister					
5. Talking to your brother and/or sister about the day's activities					
6. Spending weekends or vacations with your family					
7. Receiving compliments from your parents					
8. Visiting relatives					
9. Going to family parties					
10. Doing chores around the house					
11. Getting out of the house					
12. Going somewhere other than home after school					
13. Going places with your friends					
14. Talking with your friends					
15. Going out to eat with your friends					
16. Telling secrets to your friends					
17. Talking to your friends about the day's activities					
18. Spending weekends or vacations with your friends					
19. Going to parties with your friends					
20. Talking on the phone with your friends					
21. Writing letters to your friends					
22. Receiving letters from your friends					

	Not at all	A little	A fair amount	Much	Very much
23. Riding around in a car with your friends					
24. Going for a walk with your friends					
25. Going to the beach with your friends					
26. Going to the local spot where your friends meet					
27. Receiving compliments from a member of the same sex					
28. Interacting with people younger than you of the same sex					
29. Interacting with people younger than you of the opposite sex					
30. Interacting with people who are your own age and sex					
31. Meeting new people who are about your age					
32. Interacting with people older than you of the same sex					
33. Interacting with people older than you of the opposite sex					
34. Meeting adults					
35. Discussing school with your brother and/or sister					
36. Discussing school with your friends					
37. Going to the library					
38. Going to school					
39. Studying					
40. Receiving good grades					
41. Planning for your future					
42. Studying with your friends					
43. Participating in school sports					
44. Going to school sports events					
45. Joining school clubs or organizations					
46. Skipping school					
47. Skipping classes					
48. Interacting with people who are your age of the opposite sex					
49. Flirting with a member of the opposite sex					
50. Being noticed by a member of the opposite sex					

	Not at all	A little	A fair amount	Much	Very much
51. Receiving compliments from a member of the opposite sex					
52. Talking with a member of the opposite sex					
53. Going places with a member of the opposite sex					
54. Going out to eat with a member of the opposite sex					
55. Telling secrets to a member of the opposite sex					
56. Dating a member of the opposite sex					
57. Going steady					
58. Daydreaming about romance					
59. Kissing a member of the opposite sex					
60. Making love in a car with a member of the opposite sex					
61. Engaging in light petting with a member of the opposite sex					
62. Engaging in heavy petting with a member of the opposite sex					
63. Engaging in sexual intercourse with a member of the opposite sex					
64. Spending weekends or vacations with a member of the opposite sex					
65. Listening to music on the radio					
66. Playing records					
67. Buying records					
68. Exercising					
69. Watching television					
70. Reading a book					
71. Earning money					
72. Staying at home and relaxing					
73. Riding a bicycle					
74. Riding a motorcycle					
75. Going to bars or clubs					
76. Going to dances					
77. Going to a drive-in movie					
78. Going to work					
79. Going to plays					
80. Going to concerts					
81. Playing a musical instrument					
82. Looking nice					

	Not at all	A little	A fair amount	Much	Very much
83. Buying clothes					
84. Eating snacks					
85. Drinking nonalcoholic beverages					
86. Drinking alcoholic beverages					
87. Smoking cigarettes					
88. Smoking marijuana					
89. Taking other drugs					

90. Please write down any other experiences you particularly enjoy. ——————————

————————————————————————————————————

————————————————————————————————————

————————————————————————————————————

————————————————————————————————————

Intervention Development

Pinpointing Target Behaviors

ASSERTIVE BEHAVIOR SURVEY SCHEDULE (C and A)

RATIONALE/PURPOSE

Proper assertive behavior inevitably increases a person's self-esteem. It also prevents a build-up of anger, which can lead to various maladaptive responses such as headaches or ulcers or to aggressiveness or withdrawal.

Children and adolescents often evidence signs of nonassertive behavior patterns. The problem is compounded for them since many authority figures take a dim view of any assertive behavior on the part of young people. But liking themselves, sticking up for themselves in a reasonable way, and asking for the consideration they deserve are all good preparations for proper assertive behavior in adult life. Nonassertive patterns are learned and reinforced very early.

The Assertive Behavior Survey Schedule was developed so that the therapist can assess the degree of assertive behavior a client normally displays across a wide variety of situations with a wide variety of people.

ADMINISTRATION

The Assertive Behavior Survey Schedule should be filled out by the client. Form C should be administered by the therapist in an office setting; Form A can be filled out at home and discussed thoroughly at a later session.

GUIDELINES

1. It is helpful to point out to the client that the whole purpose of the Assertive Behavior Survey Schedule is to find out whether or not she usually stands up for herself and how strongly and appropriately.
2. In Section I, some of the items may not be worded exactly as the clients usually talk, or may even sound moralistic, preachy, or "goody-goody." However, the main concern is that each number describe a different level of assertive behavior: 1 is a good, strong assertion; 2 is a semi-assertive behavior (usually accompanied by an apology or excuse) or an inappropriate assertion; and 3 is a nonassertive behavior.
3. Also in Section I, some clients may want to know more about the details of some of the scenes presented: Is it an old person who cuts in front of me in line? Is the waitress really busy and looking exhausted and harried? If these issues are raised, it is best to tell the client not to be that specific, but to indicate, *in general,* what she would be most apt to do in that situation.
4. It may be necessary or helpful for the administrator to define some terms on the inventory, especially for younger or special needs children.

ITEM BREAKDOWN

FORM C
Number of questions: 37

Questions	Topic
I-A, I-B, I-C, IV-4, IV-7	Assertion in the face of injustice
I-D, I-E, I-F, IV-2	Assertion to get the respectful treatment deserved
I-G, All of II	Assertion with significant others
All of III, IV-9	Assertion in the face of unpleasant consequences
IV-1, IV-3, IV-5, IV-6, IV-8, IV-10	Assertion of self and the right to be seen and heard
All of V	Other assertions

FORM A

Number of questions: 41

Questions	Topic
I-B, I-C, I-D, I-F, V-4	Assertion in the face of injustice
I-A, I-E, All of IV, V-6	Assertion to get the respectful treatment deserved
I-G, I-H, I-I, All of II, V-7	Assertion with significant others
All of III, V-5, V-9	Assertion in the face of unpleasant consequences
I-J, V-1, V-2, V-3, V-8	Assertion of self and the right to be seen and heard
All of VI	Other assertions

USE OF THE INFORMATION

The information gained from the administration of the Assertive Behavior Survey Schedule is an obvious starting point for the teaching of proper assertive behavior. Before doing so, however, it is important for the therapist to inform parents or guardians of what is being taught to the child or adolescent. Some parents may not believe the child should assert herself and the new behaviors taught may be objectionable to them, thus creating problems in the child's home environment. If it is the therapist's opinion that for the child's well-being she should learn to assert herself, this rationale should be explained to the parents and permission should be granted before actual skill training is begun.

Once begun, such training can include discussion of the child's rights, role-playing, behavioral rehearsal, covert modeling (in which a client imagines watching someone else like her assert herself), covert reinforcement for proper assertive behavior, and desensitization for possible negative reactions from others when the client does finally assert herself.

Part I of the inventory can be used as a guideline for modeling by substituting a properly assertive person in the given situation instead of the client herself. Similarity of the model is important; a model of the same sex and age as the client has greater modeling power than someone of a different age or sex. Also, coping models are more effective than mastery models.

COMPARISON TO OTHER FORMS

FEAR INVENTORY: A client with many fears or one pervasive fear will usually not be assertive and may fear the consequences of assertive behavior.

PARENTAL REACTION SURVEY SCHEDULE: There may be indicators on the Assertive Behavior Survey Schedule that the child's relationship with parents or relatives is one of fear or great passivity. If child abuse is suspected, the Parental Reaction Survey Schedule may help verify the parents' feelings toward and treatment of the child.

PARENTS' AND CHILDREN'S REINFORCEMENT SURVEY SCHEDULE: Faulty interactions between parents and children as evidenced on the Assertive Behavior Survey Schedule may also appear in the assessment of how the parents and children reinforce each other.

PHYSICAL COMPLAINT SURVEY SCHEDULE: Nonassertive clients may build up resentment at injustices done to them and increase bodily tension to the point of developing headaches, stomach problems, hypertension, or other physical ailments.

SELF-EVALUATION SCALE: Several items on this scale are directly related to assertive behavior and the effect it has on self-image.

RECOMMENDED READINGS

Bornstein, M. R., Bellack, A. S., & Hersen, M. Social skills training for unassertive children: A multiple baseline analysis. *Journal of Applied Behavior Analysis,* 1977, *10,* 183–195.

Cautela, J. R. Covert reinforcement. *Behavior Therapy,* 1970, *1,* 33–50.

Cautela, J. R. Covert modeling. *Journal of Behavior Therapy and Experimental Psychiatry,* 1976, *7,* 2–16.

Elkins, D. (Ed.). *Glad to be me.* Englewood Cliffs, N. J.: Prentice-Hall, 1976.

Palmer, P. *Liking myself.* San Luis Obispo, Calif.: Impact Publishers, 1977. (a)

Palmer, P. *The mouse, the monster and me.* San Luis Obispo, Calif.: Impact Publishers, 1977. (b)

Wolpe, J. *Psychotherapy by reciprocal inhibition.* Stanford, Calif.: Stanford University Press, 1958.

ASSERTIVE BEHAVIOR SURVEY SCHEDULE (C)

Name _____ Date _____

Age _____ Sex: Boy _____ Girl _____

School _____ Grade _____

I. What would you do if these things happened to you? Circle the number that tells best what you think you would do.

   A. In the school auditorium, you are waiting in line to be seated. Someone gets in front of you.
      1. I say, "I'm sorry; I was here first" and take my seat.
      2. I say, "I'm sorry; I was here first," but let the person go ahead of me.
      3. I say nothing.

   B. In a drugstore, the clerk has been waiting on someone for about 5 minutes. He finishes and it's now your turn, but he starts to wait on someone else.
      1. I speak up and say it's my turn and then take it.
      2. I speak up and say it's my turn, but that I'll let the other person go ahead of me.
      3. I say nothing.

   C. Your father (or mother) has promised you a special trip, for example, a camping trip or an outing to an amusement park. At the last minute he or she changes his or her mind and says you are not going and doesn't give you a reason.
    For father
      1. I say, "You promised me this. Why did you change your mind? I'm really disappointed."
      2. I yell, scream, or hit something.
      3. I feel sad and go somewhere by myself and cry.
    For mother
      1. I say, "You promised me this. Why did you change your mind? I'm really disappointed."
      2. I yell, scream, or hit something.
      3. I feel sad and go somewhere by myself and cry.

   D. You are constantly being picked on or hit by another kid in your class.
      1. I say, "If you do that again, I'm warning you, I'll have to hit you back hard."
      2. I say, "Cut it out" or tell a grownup.
      3. I cry or say nothing.

   E. Your friends always decide what to do after school and don't ask you what you would like to do.
      1. I say, "Once in a while I'd like to be the one to say what we'll do."
      2. I complain, "I never get to pick what we're going to do."
      3. I say nothing and always go along with the other kids.

   F. Your lunch at the school cafeteria is badly burned or not cooked well enough.
      1. I take it back, explain what's wrong with it, and ask for another lunch.
      2. I complain to my friends about the school's food.
      3. I say nothing and eat it anyway.

   G. Your friends are making fun of someone and want you to do it with them.
      1. I tell them what they're doing is mean and to count me out.
      2. I don't say anything to my friends and stay with them while they're making fun of someone (but I don't do it).
      3. I make fun of the person my friends are making fun of.

II. What do you think will happen if you speak up for yourself to these people? Write down your answer next to each person.

   A. Mother   _____

B. Father _____

C. Brother(s) _____

D. Sister(s) _____

E. Best friend _____

F. Clerk in a store _____

G. Waiter or waitress
    in a restaurant _____

H. Friend(s) _____

I. Teacher _____

J. Your parents'
    friends _____

K. Principal _____

L. Baby-sitter _____

M. Aunts _____

N. Uncles _____

O. Cousins _____

P. Your friends'
    parents _____

Q. School bus driver _____

III. When you are afraid to speak up for yourself when someone does something that isn't fair to you, what is it that you are afraid of? Circle the letters that tell what you are afraid of.

A. I'll get yelled at.

B. I'll get hit.

C. I'll get a dirty look.

D. The person won't talk to me.

E. The person won't like me.

F. I'll feel afraid or upset.

IV. Put an X in the box that tells best how much you do each of these things.

	Not at all	A little	Very much
1. I speak up when I am right.			
2. I hit back when someone hits me.			
3. I raise my hand to ask to go to the bathroom.			
4. I don't mind asking someone to move from my place in line at school or in a store.			
5. I don't mind going into a room where other people are already sitting.			
6. I say I'm sorry for mistakes I make.			
7. I ask people to give back what they've taken from me.			
8. I raise my hand to answer the teacher's questions.			
9. I'm not afraid of feeling mad.			
10. I ask my teacher to repeat what he or she said so I'll understand.			

V. Write down your answers for these questions.

1. Please write down any other times you wish you could say or do something about what you think or feel without being afraid. _____

_____

_____

_____

_____

2. Please write down why you are afraid to speak up or do something at these times. _____

_____

_____

_____

_____

ASSERTIVE BEHAVIOR SURVEY SCHEDULE (A)

Name _____ Date _____

Age _____ Sex _____

School (if in school) _____ Grade _____

Occupation (if employed) _____

I. What would you do in the following situations? Circle the appropriate number.

A. In a restaurant, you have ordered your favorite meal. When it comes, it's not cooked to your liking.

1. You tell the waitress that it's not cooked to your taste and have her take it back and get it cooked to your liking.

2. You complain that it's not cooked to your taste, but you say you'll eat it anyway.

3. You say nothing.

B. You have been waiting in line to buy a ticket. Someone gets in front of you.

1. You say it is your turn and you get in front of him or her.

2. You say it is your turn but let the other person go before you.

3. You say nothing.

C. In the school auditorium, you are waiting in line to be seated. Someone gets in front of you.

1. You say, "I'm sorry; I was here first" and you take your seat.

2. You say, "I'm sorry; I was here first," but you let the person go ahead of you.

3. You say nothing.

D. In a drugstore, the clerk has been waiting on someone for about 5 minutes. He finishes and it's now your turn, but he starts to wait on someone else.

1. You speak up and say it's your turn and take it.

2. You speak up and say it's your turn, but that you'll let the other person go ahead of you.

3. You say nothing.

E. In a department store, the clerk has been on the phone at least 10 minutes while you are waiting.

1. You say, "Will you please wait on me now? I've been here for 10 minutes."

2. You say, "Hurry it up. I've been waiting 10 minutes."

3. You say nothing or leave.

F. Your father (or mother) has promised you a special trip, for example, a camping trip or an outing to an amusement park, or has promised to buy you something. At the last minute, he or she changes his or her mind and says you are not going or not getting what was promised you and doesn't give you a reason.

For father

1. You say, "You promised me this. Why did you change your mind? I'm really disappointed."

2. You yell, scream, or hit something.

3. You feel sad or angry and go somewhere by yourself and cry.

For mother

1. You say, "You promised me this. Why did you change your mind? I'm really disappointed."

2. You yell, scream, or hit something.

3. You feel sad or angry and go somewhere by yourself and cry.

G. Your friends are pressuring you to do something, like smoking pot, and you don't want to do it.

1. You say, "I'm not interested in doing that. I like to make my own decisions."

2. You smoke and pretend to inhale because even though you don't want to smoke pot, you don't want the kids to reject you.

3. You smoke pot with them even though you really don't want to.

H. Your friends are ridiculing or making fun of someone and expect you to join them.

   1. You tell them that what they're doing is mean and to count you out.

   2. You don't really join in the ridiculing but don't say anything to your friends and stay with them while they are doing it.

   3. You ridicule the person your friends are ridiculing.

I. You have been told by your parents to be home at midnight. At 11:30 p.m. your friends tease you to stay out with them.

   1. You say, "Sorry, I'm going home" and go.

   2. You complain about your parents' strictness, but go home.

   3. You say "OK. I'll stay out with you."

J. Someone compliments you on an item of clothing you are wearing.

   1. You say, "Thank you very much."

   2. You say, "Oh, this, I got it on sale" or "This old thing? I've had it a long time" or "It doesn't really look great on me, but it's OK."

   3. You get embarrassed and say nothing.

II. What do you think will happen if you speak up for yourself to these people? Write down your answer next to each person.

A. Mother   _____

B. Father   _____

C. Brother(s)   _____

D. Sister(s)   _____

E. Best friend   _____

F. Clerk in a store   _____

G. Waiter or waitress in a restaurant   _____

H. Friend(s)   _____

I. Teacher   _____

J. Your parents' friends   _____

K. Principal   _____

L. Aunts   _____

M. Uncles   _____

N. Cousins   _____

O. Your friends' parents   _____

P. Employer or immediate supervisor   _____

Q. Boyfriend   _____

R. Girlfriend   _____

S. School bus driver   _____

III. When you are afraid to speak up for yourself when someone does something that isn't fair to you, what is it that you are afraid of? Circle the appropriate letters.

    A. You'll be yelled at.

    B. You'll be hit.

    C. You'll be given a dirty look.

    D. The person won't talk to you.

    E. The person won't like you or will reject you.

    F. You'll feel anxious or upset.

IV. With certain important people in your life, you feel you give more than you receive. In these situations you usually:

    A. Tell the other person that you think the situation is unequal and that you expect more from them.

    B. Tend to avoid the person or give them less.

    C. Do nothing.

V. Put a check mark in the column that best describes how much you do each of the following things.

	Not at all	A little	Very much
1. I answer in class.			
2. I have no trouble going into a room where other people are already seated.			
3. I ask the teacher to repeat instructions.			
4. I ask people to move from my place in line.			
5. I'm not afraid to express my opinion even when I know people may not agree with me.			
6. I ask people to give back what they have borrowed.			
7. I say no when a group of kids is pressuring me to do something I don't want to do.			
8. I don't mind being the center of attention.			
9. I'm not afraid of feeling angry.			

VI. Write down your answers for these questions.

    1. Please write down any other situations in which you wish you could say or do something about what you think or feel without being afraid. _____

    _____

    _____

    _____

    _____

    2. Please write down why you are afraid to speak up or do something in these situations. _____

    _____

    _____

    _____

    _____

BODILY CUES FOR TENSION AND ANXIETY (C and A)

RATIONALE/PURPOSE

All clients do not experience bodily tension in exactly the same ways. For one, the stomach "turns over," while for another the back of the neck and shoulders get tight. Since the bodily experience of anxiety is different from client to client, the Bodily Cues for Tension and Anxiety inventory was developed.

ADMINISTRATION

This inventory is to be filled out by the client, with assistance given to very young children and persons with special needs. The usual administrator is the therapist, in an office setting, but it could also be administered by a parent or guardian.

GUIDELINES

1. Forms C and A each contain approximately 30 specific items which ask the client to pinpoint those areas that for him seem to be trouble spots; there are also open-ended questions to give the client the opportunity to mention any bodily cues the form may have failed to assess. These questions are placed at the end because it is likely that reading through all the items will suggest further examples of bodily tension in the client's repertoire.
2. It may be that in order to get very young children or persons with special needs to be specific, the therapist may have to help the client to imagine a thing or a situation that is aversive to produce the relevant physical cues, thus making it easier to fill out the form.
3. Another way to get clients to identify specific physical cues is to ask them to try to remember what bodily sensations they feel when they are fearful.
4. For some clients, tensing and relaxing certain parts of the body may produce embarrassment, e.g., a woman's chest or an overweight person's legs. It is important that the administrator be aware of this, since this embarrassment may produce a response that a certain area is fine and not tense at all, when in reality it is a real trouble spot.

ITEM BREAKDOWN

FORM C

Number of Questions: 32

Questions	General area	Specific area
1–4, 6	Head	Head
5		Eyes
7, 9, 18, 28		Mouth and throat
31		Neck
8	Trunk	Shoulders
16, 27		Chest
17, 19		Stomach
13	Extremities	Arms
14, 15, 30		Hands
20, 22		Legs
10, 12	General	Respiration
11, 21, 23–26, 29		General bodily sensations
32		Other sensations

FORM A

Number of questions: 34

Questions	General area	Specific area
1–4, 6	Head	Head
5		Eyes
7, 9, 18, 28		Mouth and throat
33		Neck
8	Trunk	Shoulders
16, 27		Chest
17, 19		Stomach
13	Extremities	Arms
14, 15, 31, 32		Hands
20, 22		Legs
10, 12	General	Respiration
11, 21, 23–26, 29, 30		General bodily sensations
34		Other sensations

USE OF THE INFORMATION

The findings from the Bodily Cues for Tension and Anxiety inventory are directly related to the teaching of progressive relaxation (Jacobson, 1938) in the clinical intervention setting. It is usual and desirable to teach the relaxation technique for all the muscle groups of the body, especially since those muscles that are particularly tense do in turn affect the other muscles that are not yet involved. Once a client knows the general technique, however, it is helpful for the therapist to have the results from the Bodily Cues for Tension and Anxiety inventory in order to especially focus on relaxing a client's particular trouble spots. For example, after the body has been progressively relaxed and the client is taking one long, even breath and exhaling slowly, it is helpful to have him imagine a relaxation wand slowly passing over his body from head to toe. The wand may hover (in imagery) around each particularly difficult spot and not move on until that area of the body has a very pleasant, easy, relaxed feeling of well-being.

Practice in pairing tension in one area followed by relaxation, such as a tightly clenched hand that is then relaxed, increases the probability that in the tension-producing situation, when the hand is tensed, it will then relax automatically. The client is told that when he notices the hand getting tight it indicates an increase in general tension level, and he is taught to relax the whole body when he notices this indication of tension.

COMPARISON TO OTHER FORMS

BEHAVIOR RECORD FORM: Once the areas of tension have been identified, the Behavior Record Form can be used to help the client discover the environmental components contributing to the tension (antecedents, consequences, and behavioral measurements such as frequency, intensity, and duration).

FEAR INVENTORY: In assessment, the Fear Inventory sets the stage for identifying bodily cues for tension and anxiety. Having a child imagine highly rated items on the Fear Inventory, such as a menacing dog for a child with a dog phobia, can aid greatly in pinpointing for the child the state of bodily tension that develops in a specific area in the presence of a fearful stimulus.

In the treatment area, modifying fear behavior involves specifically identifying where tension occurs in the body so that the client can substitute a relaxation response in the areas usually affected by a fear stimulus.

MEDICAL HISTORY INVENTORY: This inventory should be administered to a client who reports tension-related pain in one or several body areas.

PHYSICAL COMPLAINT SURVEY SCHEDULE: Some items on this schedule are related to bodily pain. Pain behavior should be examined to see if it is caused by tension.

RECOMMENDED READINGS

Benson, H. *The relaxation response.* New York: Morrow, 1975.

Cautela, J. R., & Groden, J. *Relaxation: A comprehensive manual for adults, children, and children with special needs.* Champaign, Ill.: Research Press, 1978.

Jacobson, E. *Progressive relaxation.* Chicago: University of Chicago Press, 1938.

Jacobson, E. *You must relax.* New York: McGraw-Hill, 1957.

Jacobson, E. *Teaching and learning: New methods for old arts.* Chicago: National Foundation for Progressive Relaxation, 1973.

Koeppen, A. Relaxation training for children. *Journal of Elementary School Guidance and Counseling,* 1974, *9*, 14–21.

BODILY CUES FOR TENSION AND ANXIETY (C)

Name _____ Date _____

Age _____ Sex: Boy _____ Girl _____

School _____ Grade _____

When you are scared of something or worried about something, you feel bad. But everyone is not the same—when some kids are worried, their stomachs feel sick; when other kids are worried, their hands shake. How does each part of *your* body feel when you are scared or worried? Put an X in the box that tells best how each part feels.

	Not at all	A little	Very much
1. My head feels light.			
2. My head aches.			
3. My head feels tight.			
4. My head feels heavy.			
5. My eyes squeeze shut.			
6. My forehead gets wrinkled.			
7. My mouth feels dry.			
8. I hold my shoulders stiffly.			
9. My mouth shuts very tightly.			
10. I can't breathe.			
11. I feel dizzy.			
12. I breathe fast.			
13. My arms get stiff.			
14. My hands shake.			
15. The insides of my hands feel wet or damp.			
16. My chest feels tight.			
17. I feel like throwing up.			
18. It's hard to swallow.			
19. My stomach feels sick or upset.			
20. My legs feel stiff.			
21. I feel like I can't move.			
22. My knees feel shaky or wobbly.			
23. I feel like I'm going to faint.			
24. I feel cold.			
25. I feel hot.			
26. I feel some of my nerves twitching. If so, where? _____			
27. My heart beats fast.			
28. I grind my teeth together.			
29. I have to go to the bathroom.			

	Not at all	A little	Very much
30. I squeeze my hands together or hold on to something tightly.			
31. My neck feels tight.			

32. What else have you noticed about your body when you are afraid or worried? Write as much as you want. _____

_____

_____

_____

_____

BODILY CUES FOR TENSION AND ANXIETY (A)

Name _____   Date _____

Age _____ Sex _____

School (if in school) _____   Grade _____

Occupation (if employed) _____

When you are afraid of or worried about something, you don't feel good. But everyone is not alike—different people feel the effects of fear in different parts of the body. How does each part of *your* body feel when you are afraid? Put a check mark in the column that best describes how each part feels.

	Not at all	A little	Very much
1. I feel light-headed.			
2. My head aches.			
3. My head feels tight.			
4. My head feels heavy.			
5. My eyes squint.			
6. I wrinkle my forehead.			
7. My mouth feels dry.			
8. I hold my shoulders stiffly.			
9. My mouth clamps shut.			
10. I can't breathe.			
11. I feel dizzy.			
12. I breathe very rapidly.			
13. My arms get stiff.			
14. My hands shake.			
15. The insides of my hands sweat or feel clammy.			
16. My chest feels tight.			
17. I feel like vomiting.			
18. A lump comes into my throat, making it difficult to swallow.			
19. I feel sick to my stomach.			
20. My legs feel stiff.			
21. I feel like I can't move.			
22. My knees feel shaky or wobbly.			
23. I feel like I'm going to faint.			
24. I feel cold.			
25. I feel hot or flushed.			
26. I feel some of my nerves twitching. If so, where? _____			
27. My heartbeat speeds up.			
28. I grind my teeth together.			
29. I feel as if I have to urinate.			
30. I feel as if I have to have a bowel movement.			

	Not at all	A little	Very much
31. I squeeze my hands together or hold onto something tightly.			
32. I dig my fingernails into my palms.			
33. My neck feels tight.			

34. What else have you noticed about your bodily reactions to tension? Write as much as you want. _____

_____

_____

_____

_____

FEAR INVENTORY (C and A)

RATIONALE/PURPOSE

In behavioral assessment the Fear Inventory constitutes an efficient method of identifying the objects and situations a client fears. It provides the client with the opportunity to indicate (in a clear, simple manner) the amount or degree of fear each item elicits upon presentation. Many children and adolescents don't like to reflect upon what they are afraid of, even (or especially!) if asked directly by a therapist. They may be more comfortable with this list, especially since it will probably contain many items that they don't fear, thus making them feel more brave.

ADMINISTRATION

This form is to be filled out by the client himself. Generally, the scale should be administered by a therapist or counselor rather than by a parent, since the child or adolescent may be inhibited from answering questions in a certain way because of perceived parental disapproval or ridicule. For very young children or for persons with special needs, assistance from an adult may be required.

GUIDELINES

1. It is suggested that at first the administrator repeatedly put each item in the context of the sentences contained in the directions so that the amount of fear may be more accurately rated. This procedure can then be faded out when it is apparent that the child understands the rating system.
2. Children often may wish to digress and discuss examples of fearful situations that a particular item calls to mind. These digressions may contain clinical cues for the therapist.

ITEM BREAKDOWN

FORM C

Number of questions: 69

Questions	Topic
4–9, 21, 25, 27, 30, 32, 33, 42*, 49	Fear of people or interactions with people
3*, 11, 20, 35, 38, 40	Fear of potentially dangerous things or situations
22, 28, 31, 34, 37, 44, 45	Fear of animals
16, 19, 26, 50, 51, 55–57, 60	Fear of assertiveness
10, 13, 24, 47	Fear of pain
1, 2, 3*, 46*, 52, 53, 54, 58, 59, 64	Fear of being left alone or of having to function independently
14, 15, 17, 29, 39, 67, 68	Fear of sensory stimuli
23, 43, 46*, 65, 66	Fear of frightening things or situations (imagery)
12, 18, 36, 41, 42*, 48, 61–63	Fear of criticism or failure
69	Other fears

FORM A

Number of questions: 64

Questions	Topic
10, 14, 16, 19, 21, 22, 31*, 32*, 55	Fear of people or interactions with people
9, 24, 27, 29, 54	Fear of potentially dangerous things or situations
11, 17, 20, 23, 26, 33	Fear of animals
6, 8, 15, 37, 38, 43, 47, 50	Fear of assertiveness
3, 5, 13, 35	Fear of pain
1, 2, 34, 39, 40–42	Fear of being left alone or of having to function independently
18, 28, 58, 59, 62, 63	Fear of sensory stimuli
12, 60, 61	Fear of frightening things or situations (imagery)
4, 7, 25, 30, 31*, 32*, 36, 44, 45, 48, 51, 56, 57	Fear of criticism or failure
46, 49, 52, 53	Fear of rejection
64	Other fears

*This indicates that the item is under more than one category.

USE OF THE INFORMATION

The administration of the Fear Inventory can help the therapist discover many fears related or unrelated to the presenting problem. These findings may become content for therapy (desensitization and covert reinforcement for coping behaviors relative to the fears). The findings may also be used as variables in several conditioning techniques involving negative imagery, e.g., covert sensitization, covert negative reinforcement, or covert response cost. However, we recommend that, as often as possible, reinforcing imagery be used with children.

It would be particularly undesirable to focus on negative imagery with a fearful child. Punishment only teaches the client what *not* to do rather than what to do. It also may have an adverse effect on the client-therapist relationship, with negative associations being made. And finally, the child or adolescent referred to the therapist is likely to have already had negative associations with other significant adults. It is desirable that the therapist be a positive social reinforcer.

Once the Fear Inventory has been administered, the therapist should list all those items checked as *Terribly afraid* (Form A) or *Really scared* (Form C) and then present them to the client for prioritizing.

COMPARISON TO OTHER FORMS

ASSERTIVE BEHAVIOR SURVEY SCHEDULE: A client with many fears or one pervasive fear will usually not be assertive and may fear the consequences of assertive behavior.

BEHAVIOR STATUS CHECKLIST (C and A): A client who indicates several behaviors that are in need of change or improvement may indicate that exaggerated fears are among those behaviors.

BODILY CUES FOR TENSION AND ANXIETY: In behavioral assessment, the Fear Inventory sets the stage for identifying bodily cues for tension and anxiety. Having a child imagine highly rated items on the Fear Inventory (e.g., a menacing dog for a child with a dog phobia) can help him pinpoint the state of bodily tension in a specific area in the presence of a frightening stimulus.

In treatment, modifying fear behavior involves identifying specifically where tension occurs in the body so that the client can learn to substitute a relaxation response in those areas when affected by a frightening stimulus.

PARENTS' AND CHILDREN'S REINFORCEMENT SURVEY SCHEDULE: Clues from this schedule regarding parent/child interaction may be related to information reported by a child on the Fear Inventory. Some items on the Inventory are directly related to parent/child interaction.

PHYSICAL COMPLAINT SURVEY SCHEDULE: For many people, fears may expand to include the area of bodily sensations, especially in those whose physical state is most often tense. Fearful bodily reactions can accompany and precipitate disease.

REINFORCEMENT SURVEY SCHEDULES: A client with a high number of reported fears will often express a low number of reinforcers in his environment. Items on the Reinforcement Survey Schedules can be used to reinforce anti-anxiety behaviors at the intervention stage.

SELF-EVALUATION SCALE: A client who has a single pervasive fear or several fears may have a poor self-image about his ability to handle crises.

RECOMMENDED READINGS

Campbell, L. M. A variation of thought-stopping in a twelve-year-old boy: A case report. *Journal of Behavior Therapy and Experimental Psychiatry,* 1974, *4,* 69–70.

Castaneda, A., McCandless, B. R., & Palermo, D. S. The children's form of the manifest anxiety scale. *Child Development,* 1956, *27,* 317–326.

Cautela, J. R. Treatment of compulsive behavior by covert sensitization. *Psychological Record,* 1966, *16,* 33–41.

Cautela, J. R. Covert negative reinforcement. *Journal of Behavior Therapy and Experimental Psychiatry,* 1970, *1,* 273–278. (a)

Cautela, J. R. Covert reinforcement. *Behavior Therapy,* 1970, *1,* 33–50. (b)

Cautela, J. R. Covert extinction. *Behavior Therapy,* 1971, *2,* 192–200.

Cautela, J. R. Covert modeling. *Journal of Behavior Therapy and Experimental Psychiatry,* 1976, *7,* 2–16. (a)

Cautela, J. R. Covert response cost. *Psychotherapy: Theory, Research and Practice,* 1976, *13,* 397–404. (b)

Cautela, J. R. Covert conditioning with children. *Journal of Behavior Therapy and Experimental Psychiatry,* 1982, *13,* 209–214.

Kanfer, F. H., Karoly, P., & Newman, A. Reduction of children's fear of the dark by competence-related and situational threat-related cues. *Journal of Consulting and Clinical Psychology,* 1975, *43,* 251–258.

Mathews, A. Fear reduction research and clinical phobias. *Psychological Bulletin,* 1978, *85,* 390–404.

Reynolds, C. R., & Richmond, B. O. What I think and feel: A revised measure of children's manifest anxiety. *Journal of Abnormal Child Psychology,* 1978, *6,* 271–280.

Sarason, S. B., Davidson, K. S., Lighthall, F. F., Waite, R. R., & Ruebush, B. K. *Anxiety in elementary school children: A report of research.* New York: Wiley, 1960.

Scherer, M. W., & Nakamura, C. Y. A fear survey schedule for children (FSS-FC): A factor analytic comparison with manifest anxiety (CMAS). *Behaviour Research and Therapy,* 1968, *6,* 173–182.

Tasto, D. L. Systematic desensitization, muscle relaxation, and visual imagery in the counter-conditioning of a four-year-old phobic child. *Behaviour Research and Therapy,* 1969, *7,* 409–411.

Weil, G. Treatment of insomnia in an eleven-year-old child through self-relaxation. *Behavior Therapy,* 1973, *4,* 282–294.

Windheuser, H. J. Anxious mothers as models for coping with anxiety. *The European Journal of Behavioral Analysis and Modification,* 1977, *2,* 39–58.

Wish, P. A., Hasazi, J. E., & Jurgela, A. R. Automated direct deconditioning of a childhood phobia. *Journal of Behavior Therapy and Experimental Psychiatry,* 1973, *4,* 279–283.

Wolpe, J., & Lang, P. J. A fear survey schedule for use in behavior therapy. *Behaviour Research and Therapy,* 1964, *2,* 27–30.

FEAR INVENTORY (C)

Name _____ Date _____

Age _____ Sex: Boy _____ Girl _____

School _____ Grade _____

All of the things listed here can make people afraid or scared. Some of them may make you really afraid; some may make you a little bit afraid; and some may not make you afraid at all! Read each thing on this list. Then decide which of these sentences is most true:

> I'm not scared of (for example, thunder) at all.
>
> I'm a little scared of _____ .
>
> I'm really scared of _____ .

Put an X in the box that tells best how you feel about the thing listed. At the end there is a question for you to answer on your own. Write as much as you want.

	Not scared at all	A little scared	Really scared
1. Being all alone by myself			
2. Being in a place I've never been before			
3. Crossing streets all by myself			
4. Being touched by my father (like getting hugs, kisses, or handshakes, or being patted on the head or back)			
5. Being touched by my mother			
6. Being touched by other people			
7. Touching my father			
8. Touching my mother			
9. Touching other people			
10. Falling down and getting hurt			
11. Riding in cars			
12. Being teased by other kids			
13. Going to the dentist			
14. Hearing thunder			
15. Seeing lightning			
16. Raising my hand to answer a question my teacher asks			
17. Hearing sirens from fire engines or alarms			
18. Getting bad marks in school			
19. Going into a room where other people are already sitting down			
20. Being in high places (like being on top of a flat roof or on a high floor of a skyscraper)			
21. Seeing people who are handicapped (like people who are blind, on crutches, or in a wheelchair)			
22. Seeing worms			

	Not scared at all	A little scared	Really scared
23. Seeing imaginary creatures (like witches or ghosts)			
24. Getting a shot from a doctor or nurse			
25. Being around strangers (people I don't know)			
26. Feeling angry (very mad)			
27. Being around people who can tell me what to do (like parents, teachers, policemen, or principals)			
28. Seeing flying insects (bugs)			
29. Hearing sudden loud noises			
30. Being around crowds of people			
31. Seeing or hearing dogs			
32. Seeing people fighting			
33. Seeing tough or mean-looking people			
34. Seeing or hearing birds			
35. Swimming in deep water			
36. Having someone look at me while I'm working			
37. Seeing dead animals			
38. Seeing guns or knives			
39. Seeing dirt			
40. Seeing fire			
41. Having someone tell me I made a mistake			
42. Doing something that makes my parents mad at me			
43. Seeing strange shapes (like shadows at night)			
44. Seeing mice			
45. Seeing harmless snakes			
46. Being all alone in the dark			
47. Seeing a doctor			
48. Making mistakes (or not being right about something)			
49. Being around older or bigger kids			
50. Asking my teacher to repeat what he or she said so I'll understand			
51. Asking someone to move from my place in line at school or in a store			
52. Leaving home to go to school			
53. Having my mother leave home to go to work or shopping or out to a party			
54. Having my father leave home to go to work or shopping or out to a party			
55. Asking to leave the room to go to the bathroom			
56. Hitting back when someone hits me			
57. Saying "I'm sorry" for a mistake I made			
58. Visiting in my friend's house			

	Not scared at all	A little scared	Really scared
59. Having my parents go away overnight			
60. Asking someone to give back what he or she has taken from me			
61. Being yelled at by a teacher or the principal in school			
62. Being yelled at by my father at home			
63. Being yelled at by my mother at home			
64. Going to some rooms in my house alone			
65. Watching scary shows on television			
66. Having bad dreams			
67. Seeing blood (my own)			
68. Seeing blood (other people's)			

69. Are there any more things that scare you? If so, use this space to write down anything else that scares you. _____

_____

_____

_____

FEAR INVENTORY (A)

Name _____ Date _____

Age _____ Sex _____

School (if in school) _____ Grade _____

Occupation (if employed) _____

The items in this questionnaire refer to things and experiences that may cause fear. Read each item. Then decide which of the following sentences is most true:

> I'm not afraid of ___(for example, being alone)___ at all.
>
> I'm slightly afraid of _____ .
>
> I'm terribly afraid of _____ .

Put a check mark in the column that best describes how you feel about that item. At the end there is a question for you to answer on your own. Write as much as you want.

	Not afraid at all	Slightly afraid	Terribly afraid
1. Being alone			
2. Being in a strange (new) place			
3. Being in an accident			
4. Being teased by others			
5. Going to the dentist			
6. Answering in class			
7. Failing in school			
8. Entering a room where other people are already seated			
9. Being in high places			
10. Seeing people who are handicapped			
11. Seeing harmless snakes			
12. Having nightmares			
13. Getting an injection from a doctor or nurse			
14. Being around strangers			
15. Feeling angry			
16. Being around people in authority			
17. Seeing insects			
18. Hearing sudden loud noises			
19. Being around crowds of people			
20. Seeing or hearing dogs			
21. Seeing people fighting			
22. Seeing tough or mean-looking people			
23. Seeing or hearing birds			
24. Swimming in deep water			
25. Being watched while working			
26. Seeing dead animals			
27. Seeing weapons (e.g., guns or knives)			

	Not afraid at all	Slightly afraid	Terribly afraid
28. Seeing dirt			
29. Seeing fire			
30. Being criticized			
31. Getting into trouble with your parents			
32. Getting into trouble with your teachers			
33. Seeing mice			
34. Being alone in the dark			
35. Seeing a doctor			
36. Making mistakes			
37. Asking your teacher to repeat instructions			
38. Asking someone to move from your place in line			
39. Leaving home			
40. Having your parents go away overnight			
41. Having your parents go away for a long vacation			
42. Going to school			
43. Asking someone to give back what he or she has taken from you			
44. Losing in a school sport			
45. Failing to get a part you tried out for in a school play			
46. Not being accepted into a club or activity			
47. Saying no when a group of people is pressuring you to do something you don't want to do			
48. Being yelled at in front of a class			
49. Having someone ignore you when you say hello			
50. Being the center of attention			
51. Losing your job			
52. Breaking up with your boyfriend or girlfriend			
53. Not being popular			
54. Becoming dependent on drugs or alcohol			
55. Becoming involved in sexual activity			
56. Being yelled at by your mother			
57. Being yelled at by your father			
58. Hearing thunder			
59. Seeing lightning			
60. Seeing imaginary creatures			
61. Seeing strange shapes (e.g., shadows at night)			
62. Seeing blood (your own)			
63. Seeing blood (other people's)			

64. Are there any other things that make you afraid? If so, use this space to list them. _____

_____

_____

MEDICAL HISTORY INVENTORY (P)

RATIONALE/PURPOSE

Some referrals of young clients may involve behavioral problems that accompany organic disease. Other referrals may be made for the specific purpose of applying behavioral principles in the treatment of an organic dysfunction, as is becoming more and more common in the field of behavioral medicine. The Medical History Inventory was developed for use in the initial data-gathering phase of such therapy. It was also developed to inventory medical symptoms for the client with a suspected but as yet undiagnosed organic dysfunction.

ADMINISTRATION

The parent or guardian who is more familiar with the young client's past and current medical history should be the person to complete this form.

Administration of the Medical History Inventory would be indicated if there were any specific concerns mentioned in the Medical History section of the more general Behavior Analysis History Questionnaire, which is administered as part of the intake procedures.

GUIDELINES

1. It is important to point out to the person filling out this inventory that she should not rely on memory alone, but should, whenever possible, check the accuracy of the data she supplies with the medical records in her possession.
2. The person completing the inventory should be told that whenever a guess is made, it should be indicated in some manner, e.g., by putting the letter *g* next to the information.

ITEM BREAKDOWN

Number of questions: 29

Questions	Topic
1–7	Prenatal history
8–15	Birth history
16–26	Early medical history
27–29	Present problems or symptoms

USE OF THE INFORMATION

The Medical History Inventory provides the therapist with a wide variety of medical background information for consideration in setting up a treatment strategy. Knowledge of the kind and number of medical problems in a client's background may suggest behavioral patterns or medical "habits" in a client's repertoire. Further, awareness of medical information is important for psychological intervention within the behavioral medicine model, which stresses the integrative concept of the relationship of psychological factors and organic functions.

The Medical History Inventory is also useful in itemizing medical symptoms for the client who may be as yet undiagnosed, and as such can serve as a step toward further referral to a medical specialist.

COMPARISON TO OTHER FORMS

BEHAVIOR ANALYSIS HISTORY QUESTIONNAIRE: This general form, an essential part of the Intake Packet, contains a small medical history section. A problem mentioned in the section might indicate a need to complete the Medical History Inventory.

BODILY CUES FOR TENSION AND ANXIETY: The Medical History Inventory should be administered to a client who reports tension-related pain in one or several areas of the body.

PARENTAL REACTION SURVEY SCHEDULE: Several items on this scale are directly related to items on the Medical History Inventory, and thus provide a good reliability check.

PHYSICAL COMPLAINT SURVEY SCHEDULE: Many physical complaints are early indicators of medical or psychological symptoms. A client with one severe or several different physical complaints should be given the Medical History Inventory.

RECOMMENDED READINGS

Cautela, J. R. *Organic dysfunction survey schedules.* Champaign, Ill.: Research Press, 1981.

Christopherson, E. R., & Rapoff, M. A. Biosocial pediatrics. In J. A. Ferguson & C. B. Taylor (Eds.), *The comprehensive handbook of behavioral medicine.* Jamaica, N. Y.: SP Medical and Scientific Books, 1980.

McNamara, J. R. (Ed.). *Behavioral approaches to medicine.* New York: Plenum, 1979.

Melamed, B. G., & Johnson, S. B. Treatment and assessment of chronic illness: Asthma and juvenile diabetes. In E. J. Mash & L. G. Terdal (Eds.), *Behavioral assessment of childhood disorders.* New York: Guilford Press, 1981.

MEDICAL HISTORY INVENTORY FOR CHILDREN AND ADOLESCENTS (P)

Name _____ Date _____

Relationship to child _____

Name of child _____ Sex _____

Age _____ Date of birth _____

School _____ Grade _____

Address _____

_____

Telephone number _____

PRENATAL HISTORY

1. Check the degree to which the child's mother had each of the following symptoms during pregnancy:

    a. Nausea

    Not at all _____ A little _____ A fair amount _____ Much _____ Very much _____

    b. Vomiting

    Not at all _____ A little _____ A fair amount _____ Much _____ Very much _____

    c. Vaginal bleeding

    Not at all _____ A little _____ A fair amount _____ Much _____ Very much _____

    d. Water retention

    Not at all _____ A little _____ A fair amount _____ Much _____ Very much _____

2. How much did the child's mother smoke during pregnancy?

    Not at all _____ A little _____ A fair amount _____ Much _____ Very much _____

3. How much did the child's mother drink alcoholic beverages during pregnancy?

    Not at all _____ A little _____ A fair amount _____ Much _____ Very much _____

4. How much weight did the child's mother gain during pregnancy? _____

5. What medications, if any, did the child's mother take during pregnancy?

Medication	Dosage	Effectiveness
_____	_____	_____
_____	_____	_____
_____	_____	_____
_____	_____	_____

6. What vitamins, if any, did the child's mother take during pregnancy?

Vitamin	Dosage	Effectiveness
_____	_____	_____
_____	_____	_____
_____	_____	_____
_____	_____	_____

7. Were there any complications due to this pregnancy? Yes _____ No _____ If so, please describe. _____

_____

BIRTH HISTORY

8. How many months pregnant was the child's mother when she gave birth? _____

9. What was the place of birth? _____

10. What was the child's weight at birth? _____ Length at birth? _____

11. How long was the child's mother in labor? _____

12. Were forceps used for the delivery? Yes _____ No _____

13. What type of delivery was it? Caesarian _____ Vaginal _____

14. Did the child's mother have any complications in the hospital before going home?

    Yes _____ No _____ If so, please describe. _____
    _____

15. Did the child have any complications in the hospital before going home?

    Yes _____ No _____ If so, please describe. _____
    _____

EARLY MEDICAL HISTORY

16. Was there any difficulty in feeding the child? Yes _____ No _____ If so, please describe. _____
    _____

17. Check any of the following problems that the child had as an infant:

    a. Allergies _____

    b. Colic _____

    c. Constipation _____

    d. Diarrhea _____

    e. Other (specify) _____

18. When did the child first walk without support? _____

19. When did the child speak his or her first word? _____

    Several words? _____

20. When was the child toilet trained? Urine _____ Stool _____

21. Check any of the following childhood illnesses that the child has had. Describe the frequency of the illness, problems the child has had with it, and how much it presently limits normal activities.

    a. Allergies _____ Describe. _____

    b. Anemia _____ Describe. _____

    c. Asthma _____ Describe. _____

    d. Chicken pox _____ Describe. _____

    e. Convulsions _____ Describe. _____

    f. Eczema _____ Describe. _____

    g. Hay fever _____ Describe. _____

    h. Measles _____ Describe. _____

    i. Meningitis _____ Describe. _____

    j. Mumps _____ Describe. _____

    k. Rheumatic fever _____ Describe. _____

    l. Rubella _____ Describe. _____

    m. Scarlet fever _____ Describe. _____

n. Tuberculosis _____ Describe. _____

o. Whooping cough _____ Describe. _____

p. Other (specify) _____

22. Has the child ever had any serious injuries? Yes _____ No _____ If so, please describe. _____
_____

23. What medications has the child taken previously?

Medication	Dosage	Dates
_____	_____	_____
_____	_____	_____
_____	_____	_____
_____	_____	_____
_____	_____	_____

24. What medications is the child taking presently?

Medication	Dosage	Date begun
_____	_____	_____
_____	_____	_____
_____	_____	_____
_____	_____	_____
_____	_____	_____

25. Has the child ever been hospitalized? Yes _____ No _____ If so, please give dates and list reasons. _____
_____

26. Does the child presently have any illnesses? Yes _____ No _____ If so, please describe. _____
_____

PRESENT PROBLEMS OR SYMPTOMS

27. Check the degree to which the child has the following problems or symptoms:

a. Hearing difficulties

Not at all _____ A little _____ A fair amount _____ Much _____ Very much _____

b. Visual problems

Not at all _____ A little _____ A fair amount _____ Much _____ Very much _____

c. Headaches

Not at all _____ A little _____ A fair amount _____ Much _____ Very much _____

d. Ear infections

Not at all _____ A little _____ A fair amount _____ Much _____ Very much _____

e. Nosebleeds

Not at all _____ A little _____ A fair amount _____ Much _____ Very much _____

f. Bleeding gums

Not at all _____ A little _____ A fair amount _____ Much _____ Very much _____

g. Toothaches

Not at all _____ A little _____ A fair amount _____ Much _____ Very much _____

h. Coughing

Not at all _____ A little _____ A fair amount _____ Much _____ Very much _____

i. Colds

   Not at all _____ A little _____ A fair amount _____ Much _____ Very much _____

j. Wheezing

   Not at all _____ A little _____ A fair amount _____ Much _____ Very much _____

k. Vomiting

   Not at all _____ A little _____ A fair amount _____ Much _____ Very much _____

l. Nausea

   Not at all _____ A little _____ A fair amount _____ Much _____ Very much _____

m. Wets bed at night

   Not at all _____ A little _____ A fair amount _____ Much _____ Very much _____

n. Wets self during the day

   Not at all _____ A little _____ A fair amount _____ Much _____ Very much _____

o. Has bowel movements in bed at night

   Not at all _____ A little _____ A fair amount _____ Much _____ Very much _____

p. Has uncontrolled bowel movements during the day

   Not at all _____ A little _____ A fair amount _____ Much _____ Very much _____

q. Has a rash or several rashes

   Not at all _____ A little _____ A fair amount _____ Much _____ Very much _____

r. Bangs his or her head

   Not at all _____ A little _____ A fair amount _____ Much _____ Very much _____

s. Rocks in bed

   Not at all _____ A little _____ A fair amount _____ Much _____ Very much _____

t. Rocks in a chair

   Not at all _____ A little _____ A fair amount _____ Much _____ Very much _____

u. Has acne

   Not at all _____ A little _____ A fair amount _____ Much _____ Very much _____

v. Drools

   Not at all _____ A little _____ A fair amount _____ Much _____ Very much _____

w. Complains of pains in the abdomen

   Not at all _____ A little _____ A fair amount _____ Much _____ Very much _____

x. Complains of pains in the arms

   Not at all _____ A little _____ A fair amount _____ Much _____ Very much _____

y. Complains of pains in the hands

   Not at all _____ A little _____ A fair amount _____ Much _____ Very much _____

z. Complains of pains in the legs

   Not at all _____ A little _____ A fair amount _____ Much _____ Very much _____

aa. Complains of pains in the feet

   Not at all _____ A little _____ A fair amount _____ Much _____ Very much _____

bb. Is hyperactive

   Not at all _____ A little _____ A fair amount _____ Much _____ Very much _____

cc. Sucks his or her thumb

   Not at all _____ A little _____ A fair amount _____ Much _____ Very much _____ dd. Tries to eat material besides food

Not at all _____   A little _____   A fair amount _____   Much _____   Very much _____

ee. Has trouble falling asleep

Not at all _____   A little _____   A fair amount _____   Much _____   Very much _____

ff. Tires easily

Not at all _____   A little _____   A fair amount _____   Much _____   Very much _____

28. Does the child eat enough?   Yes _____   No _____   Eat too much?   Yes _____   No _____

29. Please list any other physical symptoms or problems the child has. _____

_____

_____

_____

_____

_____

PARENTAL REACTION SURVEY SCHEDULE (P)

RATIONALE/PURPOSE

The Parental Reaction Survey Schedule was developed by Cautela and Brooke to assess suspected child abuse behaviors by parents and other adults in a child's environment. The nonjudgmental, data-gathering appearance of this inventory should facilitate its completion by parents who feel embarrassed or guilty about verbalizing child abuse behaviors.

ADMINISTRATION

This form is to be completed by the parent(s) directly involved in rewarding and punishing the child in question. It can be completed at home and brought to the next therapy session. It should be given to those parents who specifically ask for help in handling the discipline of their child or to those whom the therapist suspects of child abuse.

GUIDELINES

1. It is suggested that in administering this form the therapist explain to the parent that the more thoroughly he provides information, the better informed and prepared the clinician will be to provide treatment or referral.
2. The therapist should review the completed form carefully in the presence of the parent, using the form as a beginning for discussion of issues related to the nature or frequency of the discipline currently used. Once discipline practices are indicated on paper, it's often easier for the parent(s) to expand upon or clarify relevant information on this volatile topic.

ITEM BREAKDOWN

Number of questions: 30

Questions	Topic
1–3, 6, 8	Child's health
4, 5, 7, 9–12, 14, 15, 23*, 24	Parent's attitude toward child
13, 22, 27	Other significant adults' attitudes toward child
16, 17	Child's attitudes toward parents
18, 19	Parent's own punishment history
20, 21, 23*, 25, 26	Parent's discipline habits and techniques
28, 29	Parent's reasons for seeking help
30	Additional comments

*This indicates that the item is under more than one category.

USE OF THE INFORMATION

This inventory is an assessment of parental disciplinary behaviors that are suspected of being severe enough to physically and/or emotionally damage the child. As such, it can serve as a basis for referral to other therapists or support groups for stopping child abuse.

For use in private intervention, several items on the inventory investigate the thought process that occurs prior to and during the disciplining of the child. Highlighting these thoughts can aid the therapist in pointing out faulty thinking to the parent; it can also provide targets for thought-stopping on the thought(s) that precedes harsh disciplining behavior.

This form was developed in collaboration with Judd M. Brooke.

The maladaptive behaviors of the child indicated by the parent on this inventory can be decreased or extinguished using alternative methods to physical or verbal abuse. Parents can be taught time-out procedures, contingency contracting, the response cost procedure, and techniques of reinforcing desirable behaviors incompatible with the objectionable ones. Parents themselves can be desensitized to those behaviors of the child that are very aversive to them and can be taught the self-control triad (thought-stopping, relaxation, and covert reinforcement) for use when the urge to severely punish the child is elicited.

The thorough nature of the Parental Reaction Survey Schedule makes it an effective instrument in helping parents become aware of their own attitudes toward the child and toward discipline in general. For the child-abusing parent who did not *specifically* seek help with disciplining his child, the data gathered by the administration of this form may confirm what was only suspected or feared by him, and as such act as the impetus or turning point in deciding to seek help.

COMPARISON TO OTHER FORMS

ASSERTIVE BEHAVIOR SURVEY SCHEDULE: There may be indicators on this schedule that the child's relationship with parents or relatives is one of fear or great passivity.

BEHAVIOR STATUS CHECKLIST (P): A parent who indicates that a great number of behaviors of his child need to be changed may also experience difficulty with effective discipline.

HOME VISIT OBSERVATION FORM: Patterns of abuse or neglect may become apparent upon home visitation.

MEDICAL HISTORY INVENTORY: Several items on this questionnaire are directly related to items on the Parental Reaction Survey Schedule and as such provide a good reliability check.

PARENTS' AND CHILDREN'S REINFORCEMENT SURVEY SCHEDULE: Parents who find many of their child's behaviors to be objectionable will often report few reinforcing activities in their interactions with the child. The same is true for the child who fears the severely disciplining parent.

RECOMMENDED READINGS

Boisvert, M. J. The battered child syndrome. *Social Casework,* 1972, *53,* 475–480.

Burgess, R. L. Child abuse: A behavioral analysis. In B. B. Lahey & A. E. Kazdin (Eds.), *Advances in clinical child psychology* (Vol. 2). New York: Plenum, 1978.

Burgess, R. L., & Conger, R. D. Differentiating abusing and neglecting parents by direct observation of parent-child interaction. In M. L. Lauderdale, R. N. Anderson, & S. E. Cramer (Eds.), *Child abuse and neglect: Issues on innovation and implementation* (Proceedings of the Second Annual National Conference on Child Abuse and Neglect). Washington, D.C.: National Center on Child Abuse and Neglect, 1978.

Dubanowski, R. A., Evans, J. M., & Higuchi, A. A. Analysis and treatment of child abuse: A set of behavioral propositions. *Child Abuse and Neglect,* 1978, *2,* 153–172.

Friedman, R. M., Sandler, J., Hernandez, M., & Wolfe, D. A. Child abuse. In E. J. Mash & L. G. Terdal (Eds.), *Behavioral assessment of childhood disorders.* New York: Guilford Press, 1982.

PARENTAL REACTION SURVEY SCHEDULE (P)

Name of child _____ Date _____

Age _____ Sex _____ Height _____

School _____ Grade _____ Weight _____

Child's address _____

_____

Name of parent _____ Age _____

Parent's address _____
(if different)
_____

Occupation of parent _____

Name of spouse (or adult in role of spouse) _____

Address of spouse (if different from above) _____

_____

Occupation of spouse _____

List brothers and sisters of the child.

Name	Sex	Age	Living at home (yes or no)

List other people who are living in the same household as the child.

Name	Sex	Age	Relationship to child (if any)

Respond to each of the following questions, either by marking a check in the appropriate place or filling in the answer.

1. What illnesses does your child have at the present time? _____

_____

_____

2. What illnesses has your child had in the past?

Illness	Approximate date of illness

3. How often does your child get sick?

_____ Not at all   _____ A fair amount   _____ Very often

_____ A little   _____ Often

91

4. When you first found out that you were going to have (or take care of) this child you were:

	Not at all	A little	A fair amount	Much	Very much
a. Happy					
b. Sad					
c. Disappointed					
d. Fearful					
e. Angry					
f. Surprised					

5. Was a difficult pregnancy associated with this child?   Yes _____ No _____ If so, please explain.
_____
_____

6. Was the child premature?   Yes _____ No _____ If so, how premature? _____

7. Do you wish your child had been born a different sex?   Yes _____ No _____ If so, why? _____
_____
_____

8. Is the child physically handicapped?   Yes _____ No _____ If so, please describe the nature of the
handicap. _____
_____

9. Do you think your child is:

	Not at all	A little	A fair amount	Much	Very much
a. Retarded					
b. Basically mean					
c. Selfish					
d. Ugly					
e. Too fat					
f. Too thin					
g. Too short					
h. Too small					
i. Too tall					

10. How much does the child:

	Not at all	A little	A fair amount	Much	Very much
a. Interfere with your rest					
b. Interfere with your sleep					
c. Limit your freedom					
d. Burden you financially					

11. Does the child cause you embarrassment?   Yes _____ No _____ If so, in what ways? _____
_____

12. List your child's three worst faults (in order of "worst" to "better").

a. _____

b. _____

c. _____

13. If there is a spouse or other adult living in the same household as you and the child, how much do you and this person agree as to the kinds of faults that the child has?

_____ Not at all   _____ Much

_____ A little   _____ Very much

_____ A fair amount

14. List your child's three best characteristics (beginning with the best).

a. _____

b. _____

c. _____

15. How much does the child help you with household chores?

_____ Not at all   _____ Much

_____ A little   _____ Very much

_____ A fair amount

16. Whom does your child like more, you or your spouse?

_____ You   _____ Neither of you

_____ Your spouse   _____ Another person (specify) _____

_____ Both of you equally

17. Whom does your child dislike more, you or your spouse?

_____ You   _____ Neither of you

_____ Your spouse   _____ Another person (specify) _____

_____ Both of you equally

18. How did your father punish you when you were your child's age? _____

_____

_____

_____

19. How did your mother punish you when you were your child's age? _____

_____

_____

_____

20. What is the strongest discipline that you use on the child? _____

_____

_____

_____

21. What is the most effective discipline that you use on the child? _____

_____

_____

_____

22. Other than yourself, who disciplines the child?

Name	Relationship to child	Frequency of discipline
_____	_____	_____
_____	_____	_____
_____	_____	_____

23. The following is a list of behaviors that the child may exhibit. Please rate each item on a 1–5 basis for each of the questions that are asked regarding each behavior.

1 = Not at all

2 = A little (or now and then)

3 = A fair amount (or sometimes)

4 = Much (or often)

5 = Very much (or very often)

	How often does this occur?	How much does the behavior bother you?	How often do you punish the behavior?	How effective is the punishment?
a. Says no when asked to do something				
b. Cries				
c. Screams loudly				
d. Whines				
e. Won't clean room				
f. Won't pick up toys				
g. Tracks in dirt				
h. Eats in sloppy manner				
i. Urinates in pants or bed				
j. Defecates in pants or bed				
k. Takes food without permission				
l. Runs wild in house				
m. Argues with brother or sister				
n. Fights with (hits) brother or sister				
o. Tears or soils clothes				
p. Refuses to wash himself or herself				
q. Destroys property				
r. Steals				
s. Calls mother or father names				
t. Leaves home without permission				
u. Won't come home when called				
v. Won't get out of bed when called				
w. Other (specify) _____				

24. Before you punish or discipline the child, how often do you have the following thoughts? (Please rate each item on a 1–5 basis.)

1 = Not at all

2 = Now and then

3 = Sometimes

4 = Often

5 = Very often

_____ This will teach the child a lesson.

_____ This will make the child feel better.

_____ This will make me feel better.

_____ The child deserves it.

_____ The child is different.

_____ The child is stupid.

_____ This is for the child's own good.

_____ The child is bad.

_____ The child is retarded.

_____ This will teach the child to be tough.

_____ This will make him a man (or her a lady).

_____ This will make the child smarter.

_____ The child is fresh or wise.

_____ This will get the "devil" out of the child.

_____ This was done when I was a child, and it didn't hurt me any.

_____ This was done when I was a child, and it helped me.

_____ This will make the child respect me.

_____ This will make the child respect someone else.

_____ I hate (or can't stand) the child.

_____ He or she is just like his or her mother or father.

_____ The child is deliberately trying to make me feel miserable.

_____ The child is going to drive me crazy if I don't do something.

25. Please indicate how often you have used each of the following methods to change the child's behavior. Also, indicate how effective each method has been. (Please rate each item on a 1–5 basis.)

1 = Not at all

2 = A little (or now and then)

3 = A fair amount (or sometimes)

4 = Much (or often)

5 = Very much (or very often)

95

	How often	How effective
a. Spanking child's bottom		
b. Slapping child's hands		
c. Slapping child's face		
d. Hitting child with belt		
e. Hitting child with other object (specify object) _____		
f. Sending child to room		
g. Locking child in room		
h. Making child sit still in chair		
i. Tying child in chair		
j. Pulling part of child's body (for example, hair)		
k. Squeezing part of child's body		
l. Pinching part of child's body		
m. Kicking part of child's body		
n. Making child go to bed		
o. Yelling loudly at child		
p. Calling child names (for example, "stupid idiot")		
q. Ignoring child		
r. Depriving child of food		
s. Depriving child of some privilege		
t. Trying to explain why child is doing wrong		
u. Trying to explain why child is hurting others		
v. Trying to reward child when good by: 1) Giving child privileges		
2) Giving child extra money		
3) Giving child food (for example, extra dessert)		

26. Which of the child's behaviors are you most likely to severely punish? _____
_____
_____
_____

27. If there is a spouse or other adult living in the same household as you and the child, how much do you and this person agree on how to discipline the child?

_____ Not at all   _____ Much

_____ A little   _____ Very much

_____ A fair amount

28. Have you previously sought professional help in handling your child (children)? Yes _____ No _____

If so, with whom, and what was done? _____
_____
_____

29. Do you need professional help at the present time?   Yes _____ No _____ If so, why, and what do you want accomplished? _____

_____

_____

_____

30. Please make any additional comments or provide any information that you believe is relevant. Use the rest of the page if necessary.

_____

_____

_____

_____

PHYSICAL COMPLAINT SURVEY SCHEDULE (C or A)

RATIONALE/PURPOSE

For some young clients who are referred, the presenting complaint may involve an organic component, e.g., a child whose asthma has led to her manipulating her family's attention to center around herself or a child referred for maladjustment to school or peers who says he cannot control drooling or teeth grinding. Also, during the course of therapy a client may mention as an aside a physical problem such as itching eyes, headaches, or nosebleeds. In the light of such disclosures, the therapist may wish to administer the Physical Complaint Survey Schedule to ascertain to what extent the complaint occurs and/or to provide possible data for referral to a medical specialist.

ADMINISTRATION

The Physical Complaint Survey Schedule can be filled out by an adolescent at home and discussed at a later session. The therapist, however, should administer this form to children in an office setting to better clarify the child's responses or to explain some of the items.

Note that there is only one form of this schedule, not two. The same form is administered to children and adolescents.

GUIDELINES

1. It is important to explain to the client that many of the items on this inventory may happen once in a while to very healthy people: itchy skin may be due to a mosquito bite; a runny nose may be a symptom of a cold; mouth dryness may occur on a hot day; and vomiting may be caused by a 24-hour virus. For this reason, and especially with young children, it is helpful to ask "Do you know why?" if the client checks "Most of the time" for any item. For example, a child may have itchy skin because she does get a lot of insect bites. However, if the child answers "I don't know" but still reports a high degree of skin itching, the item may be significant.

2. The therapist is cautioned to be aware of the "hypochondria" reaction to this list of physical complaints, and to look for correlation between this and other data she has on the client, e.g., medical information, personal observation, and other inventories that have been filled out. Some young clients imitate parents who complain constantly about physical ailments. These clients use the complaints to draw the attention of their parents, who respond so well to physical complaints.

ITEM BREAKDOWN

Number of questions: 43

Questions	General area	Specific area
1, 32, 39	Head	Head
5, 7, 24, 36		Nose
4, 14, 26, 33		Eyes
23, 27, 37		Ears
16, 20, 21, 25, 28–31, 40		Mouth and throat
17	Trunk	Chest
41		Shoulders
2, 3, 8, 9, 42		Stomach
11	Extremities	Arms
34		Hands
10		Legs
13, 19	General	Respiration
6, 12, 15, 18, 22, 35, 38		General bodily sensations
43		Other bodily problems

USE OF THE INFORMATION

Information gleaned from the administration of this form may lead to medical diagnosis of a heretofore undisclosed organic dysfunction. However, even if a client is already aware of the reasons for a high frequency of a certain response, e.g., dizziness related to arrhythmia, the item may still be of significance for careful monitoring of the dysfunction itself and/or adjustment of medication. Therefore, it is important to carefully discuss those items rated *A lot* and to get corroboration of this rating from parents or guardians.

If after thorough evaluation (medical examination, consultation with the client's significant others, and analysis of the data in the therapist's possession) it is decided that the physical complaint arises from psychological reasons, psychological intervention may be planned. This can include reinforcement for not exhibiting the behavior, extinction of the behavior by significant others, and desensitization to antecedents that elicit the behavior.

COMPARISON TO OTHER FORMS

ASSERTIVE BEHAVIOR SURVEY SCHEDULE: Nonassertive clients may build up resentment at injustices done to them and increase bodily tension to the point of developing headaches, stomach problems, hypertension, or other physical ailments.

BODILY CUES FOR TENSION AND ANXIETY: Some items on the Physical Complaint Survey Schedule are related to bodily pain. Pain behavior should be examined as to the possibility of its being tension-related.

FEAR INVENTORY: It is possible that some of the items on the Physical Complaint Survey Schedule may occur in the presence of a phobic stimulus, e.g., a child with a dog phobia may develop a dry mouth when facing a menacing dog. Also, fearful bodily reactions can accompany and precipitate disease.

MEDICAL HISTORY INVENTORY: Many physical complaints are early indicators of medical symptoms. A client with one severe or several different physical complaints should be given the Medical History Inventory.

RECOMMENDED READINGS

Cautela, J. R. Covert reinforcement. *Behavior Therapy,* 1970, *1,* 33–50.

Cautela, J. R. Covert extinction. *Behavior Therapy,* 1971, *2,* 192–200.

Cautela, J. R. *Organic dysfunction survey schedules.* Champaign, Ill.: Research Press, 1981.

Gentry, D. Compliance with medical regimes. In R. B. Williams & W. D. Gentry (Eds.), *Behavioral approaches to medical treatment.* Cambridge, Mass.: Ballinger, 1977.

Knapp, T. J., & Peterson, L. W. Behavior management in medical and nursing practice. In W. E. Craighead, A. E. Kazdin, & M. J. Mahoney (Eds.), *Behavior modification: Principles, issues and applications.* Boston: Houghton-Mifflin, 1976.

Melamed, B. G., & Siegel, L. J. Management of childhood disorders. In *Behavioral medicine: Practical applications in health care.* New York: Springer, 1980.

PHYSICAL COMPLAINT SURVEY SCHEDULE (C or A)

Name ————————————————————————— Date ———————————————

Age ————— Sex —————

School ————————————————————————— Grade ———————————————

Physician's name, address, and telephone number —————————————————————————

Put a check mark in the column that tells best how often you have each of the following problems with your body.

	Not at all	Sometimes	Most of the time
1. I have headaches.			
2. I get sick to my stomach.			
3. I feel hungry after eating.			
4. My eyes itch.			
5. My nose itches.			
6. My skin itches.			
7. My nose runs or leaks.			
8. I throw up.			
9. My stomach hurts me.			
10. My legs hurt.			
11. My arms hurt.			
12. I sweat when it's not hot in my house or outside.			
13. I have trouble breathing.			
14. I have trouble seeing.			
15. I get tired easily.			
16. I get thirsty.			
17. I get pains in my chest.			
18. I bump into things.			
19. It hurts me to breathe.			
20. My mouth gets dry.			
21. I drool over my chin.			
22. I get dizzy.			
23. I hear ringing in my ears.			
24. I sneeze.			
25. My throat hurts.			
26. When my eyes are open, I have trouble seeing anything.			
27. I have trouble hearing.			
28. My gums bleed.			
29. My teeth ache.			
30. I bite my tongue.			

	Not at all	Sometimes	Most of the time
31. I grind my teeth (bite down on my teeth and rub them back and forth against each other) when I'm not eating.			
32. My head itches.			
33. My eyes water.			
34. My hands shake.			
35. It hurts when I go to the bathroom.			
36. My nose bleeds.			
37. My ears hurt.			
38. I wake up in the middle of the night.			
39. My face gets hot.			
40. I have trouble swallowing.			
41. My shoulders get tight.			
42. I don't feel hungry when it's time to eat.			

43. Please list any other problems you often have with your body. _____

_____

_____

_____

_____

_____

SCHOOL BEHAVIOR STATUS CHECKLIST (S)

RATIONALE/PURPOSE

School staff members sometimes have difficulty in identifying specifically which behaviors are problematic for the student. A child may exhibit some behaviors in one situation and not in another. The School Behavior Status Checklist was developed to assist the staff in determining the frequency and duration of adaptive and maladaptive behaviors emitted in the school environment. Each staff member involved is asked to rate the behaviors in terms of importance to target for change; the checklist also helps clarify which behaviors are situation-specific and which are present in a number of situations. This gives the therapist or school counselor a starting point in deciding which behaviors will be observed and who would be best suited to do the observations. The questions are stated in the positive to encourage the identification of those areas in which the child is behaving appropriately and/or skillfully. A 5-point scale has been used to increase specificity.

ADMINISTRATION

The School Behavior Status Checklist should be filled out by those who play a significant role in the child's life within the school environment. Each staff member involved should fill out the form independently. A person skilled in behavioral techniques, such as a consulting therapist or a school counselor, is usually the one who compiles the information and recommends the next step.

GUIDELINES

The *Need to Change* category should be determined by the staff member's professional opinion of which behaviors are causing the child difficulty, as well as which behaviors are causing the staff member and other children difficulty (often these are one and the same).

ITEM BREAKDOWN

Number of questions: 61

Questions	Topic
1, 2, 10, 58*	Attentional behaviors
6, 23*, 30, 32, 34, 36, 37*, 38, 40–42, 52*	Social behaviors
7, 9, 11, 12, 13, 18, 26, 47, 51*, 58*	Compliance behaviors
3, 4, 5, 8, 14–17, 20, 22, 23*, 35, 43–46, 48, 51*	Responsibility/self-control behaviors
19, 24, 25, 29, 31, 33, 37*, 39, 52*, 53*, 54*, 55–57	Adaptive/relaxed functioning
21, 27, 28	Age- and sex-appropriate behaviors
49, 50, 53*, 54*	Academic skills
59	Student's greatest assets
60	Student's greatest liabilities
61	Other behaviors

ADDENDUM FOR ADOLESCENTS

Number of questions: 5

Questions	Topic
62–66	Responsibility/self-control behaviors

*This indicates that the item is under more than one category.

USE OF THE INFORMATION

This form aids the identification of behavioral strengths and weaknesses and suggests to the professional working with the youngster which behaviors might be targeted for observation and treatment. The staff's perception of the child or adolescent is also clarified.

Ratings of 1s and 2s in the *Behavior Occurs* category and 4s and 5s in the *Need to Change* category should be compiled and prioritized within each category. The following areas need to be considered when prioritizing:

1. Which behavior changes would be most beneficial for the child?
2. Which behavior changes would be most beneficial for the improvement of the relationship of the child to staff members and/or to other children?
3. Which behavior changes are most easily achievable? (Those in the program need positive feedback early in the process in order to keep working.)
4. In terms of shaping, which behaviors are prerequisites for which other behaviors?

Once the target behaviors have been established, behavioral observation and intervention can take place.

COMPARISON TO OTHER FORMS

BEHAVIOR RECORD FORM: Use of the Behavior Record Form is the next step in the behavioral analysis process after administration of the School Behavior Status Checklist.

BEHAVIOR STATUS CHECKLISTS: It may be helpful to the therapist to determine what the youngster considers problematic in his life, and the input of the parents also can be a useful adjunct in the school programming.

BEHAVIORAL RATING CARD: Once the problem areas have been decided upon, the Behavioral Rating Card provides an easy method of programming for a child within the school environment.

GUIDELINES FOR TIME-OUT: The time-out procedure can be applied once the behaviors to be targeted for change have been ascertained.

HOME VISIT OBSERVATION FORM: Often problematic behaviors in the school environment are also problematic at home. In selecting behaviors for change, the knowledge of which behaviors are problems at home can be very helpful.

RESPONSE COST SURVEY SCHEDULE: Response cost items may be utilized in the school environment once target behaviors have been identified.

SCHOOL REINFORCEMENT SURVEY SCHEDULE: After using the School Behavior Status Checklist to decide on behaviors to be targeted, the assessment of potential reinforcers with this form is an important step.

SELF-EVALUATION SCALE: In evaluating a child or adolescent for school problems, it is important to know how he sees himself, as well as how school personnel see him.

SESSION REPORT: The therapist, as an agent of change, needs to connect what is going on for the child in school with the weekly developments in therapy.

RECOMMENDED READINGS

Refer to the Behavior Status Checklist (C and A), Recommended Readings section.

SCHOOL BEHAVIOR STATUS CHECKLIST (S)

Name of student _____ Date _____

Person describing student _____

Title/relationship to student _____

Amount of time spent with student during school week _____

Length of time have known student _____

School _____ Grade of student _____

Circle the number in the first column that ⸍ ⸍describes how often the student performs the listed behavior and circle the number in the second ⸍ indicates the degree to which you would like the frequency of the behavior to change.

						/s		Need to Change			
1. Completes tasks or ar						5		1 2 3 4 5			
2. Works within time ⸍					4	5		1 2 3 4 5			
3. Refrains from ma'					4	5		1 2 3 4 5			
4. Raises his or her hanʼ				3	4	5		1 2 3 4 5			
5. Stays in his or her seat wheʼ				3	4	5		1 2 3 4 5			
6. Participates in extracurricular schoʼ			2	3	4	5		1 2 3 4 5			
7. Does what he or she is told			2	3	4	5		1 2 3 4 5			
8. Gets attention in appropriate ways		1	2	3	4	5		1 2 3 4 5			
9. Leaves the room only with permission		1	2	3	4	5		1 2 3 4 5			
10. Pays attention when given instructions		1	2	3	4	5		1 2 3 4 5			
11. Follows instructions		1	2	3	4	5		1 2 3 4 5			
12. Does what he or she is told without crying or tantrum behavior		1	2	3	4	5		1 2 3 4 5			
13. Does what he or she is told without arguing or talking back		1	2	3	4	5		1 2 3 4 5			
14. Has adequate eating and table manners in the cafeteria		1	2	3	4	5		1 2 3 4 5			
15. Is clean and well-groomed		1	2	3	4	5		1 2 3 4 5			
16. Has control of bowel movements		1	2	3	4	5		1 2 3 4 5			
17. Has bladder control		1	2	3	4	5		1 2 3 4 5			
18. Does homework		1	2	3	4	5		1 2 3 4 5			
19. Accepts failure well		1	2	3	4	5		1 2 3 4 5			
20. Refrains from complaining about physical symptoms		1	2	3	4	5		1 2 3 4 5			
21. Makes age-appropriate decisions		1	2	3	4	5		1 2 3 4 5			
22. Protects himself or herself from physical injury		1	2	3	4	5		1 2 3 4 5			
23. Laughs at appropriate times		1	2	3	4	5		1 2 3 4 5			
24. Spends time alone		1	2	3	4	5		1 2 3 4 5			
25. Handles new situations well		1	2	3	4	5		1 2 3 4 5			

	Behavior Occurs	Need to Change
26. Attends school regularly	1 2 3 4 5	1 2 3 4 5
27. Exhibits gender-appropriate behaviors	1 2 3 4 5	1 2 3 4 5
28. Exhibits sexual behavior appropriate to age	1 2 3 4 5	1 2 3 4 5
29. Appears confident he or she will succeed	1 2 3 4 5	1 2 3 4 5
30. Spends time with friends	1 2 3 4 5	1 2 3 4 5
31. Feels comfortable about		
a. being in school	1 2 3 4 5	1 2 3 4 5
b. being with other students	1 2 3 4 5	1 2 3 4 5
c. being in new situations	1 2 3 4 5	1 2 3 4 5
d. being taught new subject matter	1 2 3 4 5	1 2 3 4 5
e. group activities in the classroom	1 2 3 4 5	1 2 3 4 5
32. Makes friends easily	1 2 3 4 5	1 2 3 4 5
33. Makes positive statements about himself or herself	1 2 3 4 5	1 2 3 4 5
34. Gets along well with peers	1 2 3 4 5	1 2 3 4 5
35. Responds well to criticism	1 2 3 4 5	1 2 3 4 5
36. Smiles	1 2 3 4 5	1 2 3 4 5
37. Plays solitary games	1 2 3 4 5	1 2 3 4 5
38. Plays games involving others	1 2 3 4 5	1 2 3 4 5
39. Has a good sense of humor	1 2 3 4 5	1 2 3 4 5
40. Is a good sport	1 2 3 4 5	1 2 3 4 5
41. Shares with others	1 2 3 4 5	1 2 3 4 5
42. Handles competitive situations well	1 2 3 4 5	1 2 3 4 5
43. Tells the truth	1 2 3 4 5	1 2 3 4 5
44. Respects the property of others	1 2 3 4 5	1 2 3 4 5
45. Asks permission before using another person's possessions	1 2 3 4 5	1 2 3 4 5
46. Refrains from the use of violence		
a. in the classroom	1 2 3 4 5	1 2 3 4 5
b. at recess	1 2 3 4 5	1 2 3 4 5
c. in the cafeteria and hallways	1 2 3 4 5	1 2 3 4 5
d. in unstructured situations	1 2 3 4 5	1 2 3 4 5
47. Follows the rules for		
a. the classroom	1 2 3 4 5	1 2 3 4 5
b. recess	1 2 3 4 5	1 2 3 4 5
c. the school at large	1 2 3 4 5	1 2 3 4 5
48. Keeps hands to himself or herself	1 2 3 4 5	1 2 3 4 5
49. Performs to ability in		
a. reading	1 2 3 4 5	1 2 3 4 5
b. math	1 2 3 4 5	1 2 3 4 5
c. science	1 2 3 4 5	1 2 3 4 5
d. social studies	1 2 3 4 5	1 2 3 4 5
e. language	1 2 3 4 5	1 2 3 4 5
f. physical education	1 2 3 4 5	1 2 3 4 5

	Behavior Occurs	Need to Change
50. Performs at grade level or above in		
a. reading	1 2 3 4 5	1 2 3 4 5
b. math	1 2 3 4 5	1 2 3 4 5
c. science	1 2 3 4 5	1 2 3 4 5
d. social studies	1 2 3 4 5	1 2 3 4 5
e. language	1 2 3 4 5	1 2 3 4 5
51. Acts appropriately when taken on field trips and outside activities	1 2 3 4 5	1 2 3 4 5
52. Appears relaxed in social situations	1 2 3 4 5	1 2 3 4 5
53. Volunteers questions or information in the classroom	1 2 3 4 5	1 2 3 4 5
54. Answers questions when called on	1 2 3 4 5	1 2 3 4 5
55. Appears relaxed in the classroom	1 2 3 4 5	1 2 3 4 5
56. Has consistent moods	1 2 3 4 5	1 2 3 4 5
57. Spends an appropriate amount of time in the nurse's office	1 2 3 4 5	1 2 3 4 5
58. Starts tasks when told	1 2 3 4 5	1 2 3 4 5

59. The student's greatest assets are:

    a. _____

    b. _____

    c. _____

    d. _____

60. The student's greatest liabilities are:

    a. _____

    b. _____

    c. _____

    d. _____

61. Please list any other relevant behaviors about this student that this checklist brought to mind. Rate how often each behavior occurs and how much you feel it needs to be changed, using the same 5-point scale you used to rate the previous behaviors. _____

_____

_____

_____

_____

ADDENDUM FOR ADOLESCENTS

	Behavior Occurs	Need to Change
62. Refrains from swearing	1 2 3 4 5	1 2 3 4 5
63. Refrains from drug use	1 2 3 4 5	1 2 3 4 5
64. Refrains from the use of obscene language	1 2 3 4 5	1 2 3 4 5
65. Has friends that are a good influence	1 2 3 4 5	1 2 3 4 5
66. Refrains from the use of alcohol	1 2 3 4 5	1 2 3 4 5

SELF-EVALUATION SCALE (C and A)

RATIONALE/PURPOSE

Poor self-image is a common label often used by professionals when referring a client for treatment. The list of statements contained in the Self-Evaluation Scale operationally defines the term *self-image,* breaking it down to certain behaviors that can be manipulated. The items are worded positively, e.g., "I am good" rather than "I am bad" or "Most of the time I feel nice and relaxed" rather than "Most of the time I feel tight and tense." This format exemplifies good modeling technique based on the vicarious learning data out of the learning laboratories. It teaches what behavior is desirable rather than teaching what is undesirable.

ADMINISTRATION

Both forms are to be filled out by the client, with perhaps some assistance given to very young children or persons with special needs. Except under unusual circumstances, adolescents should easily be able to complete the Self-Evaluation Scale (Form A). It is suggested that the Self-Evaluation Scale (Form C) be administered in an office setting overseen by a therapist. However, when the therapist considers it appropriate, Form C can be administered by a parent or guardian at home.

GUIDELINES

1. The therapist should be aware that the client may desire to "please the therapist," not wanting to admit anything is not perfect or good about herself. This is often true of very young children. In this instance, the therapist might say, "I really want to know what you feel about these things," creating a warm, empathic climate.
2. The client may feel that she needs help so much that every item is rated very low to give evidence of how much she needs counseling.
3. The therapist should be aware of the common problem of sharp self-criticism by adolescents.
4. It may be helpful to have more than one administration for adolescents, because of their tendency toward mood swings. Repeated administrations within a short period of time may show them how labile they are and also provide more reliable information for the therapist.
5. The therapist might want to ask the client about sharing information from the Self-Evaluation Scale with other professionals, if that is thought to be helpful. He might say, "This information is basically for me; is there anyone else you'd like me to share it with, or would you rather not? Or would you feel better able to fill this out if I promised not to tell anyone about the information?"

ITEM BREAKDOWN

FORM C
Number of questions: 47

Questions	Topic
15, 16, 18–21, 23–28	Perception of how others view him or her
1, 3, 12, 14	Perception of overall self-worth
6, 10, 11, 13, 30, 32, 36, 40	Adaptive functioning
31, 41–45	Body image
2, 33–35	Perception of own learning ability
4, 5, 9, 22, 29, 39	Self-confidence
7, 8, 17, 37, 38	Perception of own social skills
46	Most-liked characteristics
47	Least-liked characteristics

FORM A

Number of questions: 44

Questions	Topic
14–17, 19–24, 37	Perception of how others view him or her
1, 10, 12, 13	Perception of overall self-worth
4, 8, 9, 11, 18, 25, 27, 32, 35	Adaptive functioning
38–42	Body image
28–31	Perception of own learning ability
2, 3, 7	Self-confidence
5, 6, 33, 34, 36	Perception of own social skills
43	Most-liked characteristics
44	Least-liked characteristics

USE OF THE INFORMATION

Invariably an individual esteems one characteristic of herself over another. One client may value intelligence over appearance, while another may value appearance over intelligence. A preference for certain characteristics also may change over time within the same individual. For instance, an adolescent may value an attractive appearance more highly now than when she was 7 years old.

When this form is used for assessment, the overall self-image can be more specifically related to the amount of reinforcement in the client's environment, and often to the degree of severity and the duration of the presenting complaint. A negative self-evaluation on certain items might suggest an intervention such as inserting positive self-statements (as contained in this scale) into a procedure that utilizes positive imagery. At any rate, it is more helpful and to the point to say of a client "X says she doesn't get along well with people" than to say "X has a poor self-image." The former statement suggests social skills training might help, while the latter is too abstract a concept to work with, making both the therapist and client feel helpless.

The therapist is cautioned not to assume an ongoing or pervasive poor self-concept on the client's part on the basis of one administration. The nature and intensity of the presenting complaint may be such as to affect the client's perception in a general way and to reduce drastically the reinforcing effects of her environment. For instance, a child with a dog phobia may say other people don't like her because they express impatience with her fear manifestations. Upon successful therapeutic intervention, rating scale results may improve dramatically, indicating that the maladaptive behavior caused the poor self-concept and not vice versa.

COMPARISON TO OTHER FORMS

ASSERTIVE BEHAVIOR SURVEY SCHEDULE: Invariably, a client who is unable to be properly assertive lacks self-esteem.

BEHAVIOR STATUS CHECKLIST: A client who lists several behaviors as needing change or improvement may express a poor self-evaluation.

FEAR INVENTORY: A client who has a single pervasive fear or several fears may have a poor self-image of her ability to handle crises.

REINFORCEMENT SURVEY SCHEDULES: A poor self-image is often related to lack of reinforcement in a client's environment.

SCHOOL BEHAVIOR STATUS CHECKLIST: If the client perceives that some of her school behaviors are a problem, she may express a poor self-evaluation.

RECOMMENDED READINGS

Cautela, J. R. Covert reinforcement. *Behavior Therapy,* 1970, *1,* 33–50.

Cautela, J. R., & Brion-Meisels, L. A children's reinforcement survey schedule. *Psychological Reports,* 1979, *44,* 327–338.

Cautela, J. R., & Cautela, J. H-A-B-I-T rating scale. In J. R. Cautela, *Behavior analysis forms for clinical intervention* (Vol. 2). Champaign, Ill.: Research Press, 1981.

Cautela, J. R., & Kastenbaum, R. A reinforcement survey schedule for use in therapy, training, and research. *Psychological Reports,* 1967, *20,* 1115–1130.

Cautela, J. R., & Upper, D. The behavioral inventory battery: The use of self-report measures in behavioral analysis and therapy. In M. Hersen & A. S. Bellack (Eds.), *Behavioral assessment: A practical handbook.* Elmsford, N. Y.: Pergamon Press, 1976.

Cautela, J. R., & Upper, D. Behavioral analysis, assessment and diagnosis. In D. Upper (Ed.), *Perspectives in behavior therapy.* Kalamazoo, Mich.: Behaviordelia, 1977.

Cautela, J. R., & Wisocki, P. The thought-stopping procedure: Description, application, and learning theory interpretations. *Psychological Record,* 1977, *2,* 225–264.

Coopersmith, S. *The antecedents of self-esteem.* San Francisco: W. H. Freeman, 1967.

Dewhurst, D. L. T., & Cautela, J. R. A proposed reinforcement survey schedule for special needs children. *Journal of Behavior Therapy and Experimental Psychiatry,* 1980, *11,* 109–112.

Lowe, M. R., & Cautela, J. R. A self-report measure of social skill. *Behavior Therapy,* 1978, *9,* 535–544.

SELF-EVALUATION SCALE (C)

Name _____ Date _____

Age _____ Sex: Boy _____ Girl _____

School _____ Grade _____

Read each sentence out loud. You will probably feel different about each sentence. Here are some of the ways you may feel after reading a sentence:

> That is *not at all* true.
>
> That is true *a little*.
>
> That is *very much* true.

Put an X in the box that tells best how you feel about the sentence you just read. At the end there are two questions for you to answer on your own. Write as much as you want.

	Not at all	A little	Very much
1. I am good.			
2. I am smart.			
3. I am someone special.			
4. I can do anything I really try to do.			
5. When a problem comes up, I can handle it.			
6. Most of the time I feel nice and relaxed.			
7. I am nice to people.			
8. I like the way I act around people.			
9. I can control myself.			
10. I laugh when things are funny.			
11. I am happy.			
12. I tell the truth.			
13. I like to help people.			
14. I am generous.			
15. People like me.			
16. People like to be with me.			
17. I get along very well with people.			
18. People can learn things from me.			
19. People can be happy I'm around.			
20. People tell me secrets.			
21. People believe what I say.			
22. I am right when I believe things about people.			
23. Other people tell me their troubles.			
24. People think I'll always do what I promise to do.			
25. People think I'm a good friend.			
26. People at school like me.			
27. People in my neighborhood like me.			
28. My family likes me.			
29. I can do my work in school.			

	Not at all	A little	Very much
30. I like my work in school.			
31. I like the way I look.			
32. I believe other people when they tell me things.			
33. I feel smart enough.			
34. I can read well enough.			
35. I think I've learned a lot in school.			
36. It doesn't bother me too much when people tell me something is wrong with me or I've done something wrong.			
37. I know how to love people.			
38. I am a good friend.			
39. I can help people.			
40. I think about the good parts of things, not the bad.			
41. I like the way my face looks.			
42. I like the way my body looks from the neck down.			
43. I like the way my hair looks.			
44. I like how tall I am.			
45. I like the way my fingernails look.			

46. What I like best about myself is _____

_____

_____

_____

_____

47. What I like least about myself is _____

_____

_____

_____

_____

SELF-EVALUATION SCALE (A)

Name ——————————————————————————— Date ——————————————

Age ————— Sex —————

School (if in school) ——————————————————— Grade ——————————

Occupation (if employed) ————————————————————————————————

Read each item. You will probably feel different about each one. Here are some of the ways you may feel after reading an item:

> That is *not at all* true.
> That is true *a little.*
> That is *very much* true.

Put a check mark in the column that best describes how you feel about that item. At the end there are two questions for you to answer on your own. Write as much as you want.

	Not at all	A little	Very much
1. I am a worthwhile person.			
2. I feel confident.			
3. I speak up when I'm right.			
4. I am calm and relaxed.			
5. I am nice to other people.			
6. I like the way I behave with people.			
7. I feel I have control of my actions.			
8. I have a good sense of humor.			
9. I am a happy person.			
10. I am an honest person.			
11. I like to help people.			
12. I am satisfied with my accomplishments up to the present time.			
13. I am an unselfish person.			
14. Generally I am liked.			
15. People find me enjoyable to be with.			
16. People tell me their problems.			
17. People trust me.			
18. I am usually right in my judgment of people.			
19. People have confidence in me.			
20. People think I am true to my word.			
21. People think they can count on me.			
22. My friends appreciate me.			
23. People at school like me.			
24. My family appreciates me.			
25. I like school.			
26. I like the way I look.			
27. I trust people.			

	Not at all	A little	Very much
28. I feel that I'm intelligent.			
29. My reading ability is satisfactory.			
30. My knowledge of current events is adequate.			
31. I am satisfied with what I've learned in school so far.			
32. I can handle criticism well.			
33. I am able to love others.			
34. I am a good friend to others.			
35. I usually look at the bright side of things.			
36. I like the way I act in social situations.			
37. People like to have me around.			
38. I like the way my face looks.			
39. I like my body build from the neck down.			
40. I am satisfied with the general appearance of my hair.			
41. I like my height.			
42. I like the way my fingernails look.			

43. What I like best about myself is _____

_____

_____

_____

_____

44. What I like least about myself is _____

_____

_____

_____

_____

Discovering Reinforcers

PARENTS' AND CHILDREN'S REINFORCEMENT SURVEY SCHEDULE (P, C, and A)

RATIONALE/PURPOSE

The Parents' and Children's Reinforcement Survey Schedule forms were developed to assess the reinforcing activities parents and their children usually enjoy together. The forms are reciprocal, with many overlapping items. Thus, by the administration of these forms to both parents and child, it is possible for the therapist to discover if a child finds an activity such as talking to her mother as pleasant as the mother finds talking to the child.

ADMINISTRATION

Forms P and A can be completed by the appropriate party at a convenient time and brought to the next counseling session. To help in the clarification of certain items, it is suggested that Form C be filled out by the child in the presence of the therapist, not the parent. This is recommended so that the child will not be influenced on the rating of certain items by parental disappointment or pressure.

It is generally advised that when Forms C and A are administered, Form P also be filled out, so that the reciprocal relationship can be noted.

GUIDELINES

1. Form C has only a 3-point rating system for each item, as opposed to Forms P and A which each have a 5-point rating system. The shorter system on Form C facilitates the rating of degree of reinforcement for younger clients.
2. On Form P the word *child* is used on each item; this term refers both to children and adolescents. One term was used for ease in reading, but refers to the parents' offspring regardless of chronological age.
3. For the purposes of family therapy, both parents should each fill out a copy of Form P for each child involved in therapy. However, each child need only fill out one copy of the inventory, since items are already differentiated for mother and father.
4. On Forms A and C, it is recommended that the information pertinent to both parents be provided, even if one parent is partially or totally absent from the child's environment through separation or divorce.
5. In some special cases, information should be provided on interactions with stepfathers and stepmothers. It should be clearly labeled for the therapist as information about a stepparent.

ITEM BREAKDOWN

FORM P

Number of questions: 34

Questions	Topic
1–12	Activities directly involving interaction with child
13–27	Activities involving parallel enjoyment with child
28–33	Activities related to child
34	Other activities

FORM C

Number of questions: 27

Questions	Topic
1-10	Activities directly involving interaction with parent
11-23	Activities involving parallel enjoyment with parent
24-26	Activities related to parent
27	Other activities

FORM A

Number of questions: 28

Questions	Topic
1-9	Activities directly involving interaction with parent
10-23	Activities involving parallel enjoyment with parent
24-27	Activities related to parent
28	Other activities

USE OF THE INFORMATION

In therapy involving a whole family, these forms are invaluable in helping the individuals focus on those aspects of their interactions they *do* find pleasurable. One cause of depression (behaviorally speaking) for individuals may be a lack of positive reinforcement. Similarly, a breakdown in pleasant family relations can be viewed as a lack of reciprocal reinforcement among family members. Thus, for the assessment phase of behavioral family therapy, these forms are very useful.

The three inventories provide immediate data to clients, who are often surprised at the small number of reinforcing interactions they normally engage in. The data can be used by the therapist to point out to the clients an operational definition of their family problems—lack of positive interactions.

In the treatment phase, some of the positively stated behaviors on these inventories can become target behaviors to be increased by overt or covert reinforcement or contingency contracting. By becoming aware of the reinforcing aspects of parent-child interactions, the therapist can reinforce these behaviors and encourage a higher frequency of reinforcing interactions. Besides becoming target behaviors, the highly rated items on these inventories can become scenes for overt or covert reinforcement for other behaviors that should be increased.

For children, whose environment is normally more closely tied to parents than the environment of the adolescent, the highly rated items can be used as reinforcing imagery in applying covert reinforcement to increase almost any behavior. Use of an item from these inventories rather than from the more general Reinforcement Survey Schedules may be indicated for a child who has a presenting complaint not related to the family, e.g., a fear of injections, but who also experiences faulty interactions with parents. Use of the reinforcing aspects of interaction with parents (as assessed by these forms) as reinforcing scenes may also increase the child's positive regard for her relations with her parents.

For adolescents who may have experienced total breakdown in communication with parents before coming to therapy, finding out what things they *do* enjoy doing with parents (no matter how few) is one way of gradually reintroducing parental-adolescent interaction into the family lifestyle.

For parents, the positively stated items on Form P provide a format for finding the positive aspects of interaction with their children, which is the first step toward positive interaction. Indeed, all three forms provide a stimulus for looking at the relationship positively.

Finally, the forms may contain clinical cues in the treatment of the child with one deceased or totally absent parent who has sanctified all interactions with the missing parent with a halo effect. A special administration of Form C or A may be helpful in such cases. It can provide the therapist and remaining parent with data to confirm or deny clinical hunches on how the child is thinking, and possibly, at the right time in therapy, the data can be provided to the child to point out this halo effect in her recollection of the missing parent.

COMPARISON TO OTHER FORMS

ASSERTIVE BEHAVIOR SURVEY SCHEDULE: Several items on this scale help diagnose faulty interactions between parents and children.

FEAR INVENTORY: Some items on this scale are directly related to interactions between parents and children.

GUIDELINES FOR PARENTAL DISCIPLINE: Parents may find that interactions between themselves and their child that the child has noted as reinforcing may be used as positive consequences in their discipline program.

PARENTAL REACTION SURVEY SCHEDULE: This inventory provides clues for possible patterns of child abuse. Correlation of this form with the Parents' and Children's Reinforcement Survey Schedule can further the assessment of such suspected behavior.

REINFORCEMENT MENU: Reinforcing activities that parents and children perform together may also fulfill the criterion of immediate availability to the client, thus becoming items to be added to the Reinforcement Menu.

REINFORCEMENT SURVEY SCHEDULES: These more general scales have correlative items on the scales that assess reinforcing parent-child interactions.

SCHOOL REINFORCEMENT SURVEY SCHEDULE: All the reinforcement survey schedules are related, although some (as this school scale) are for a particular setting. Often related items appear from schedule to schedule.

RECOMMENDED READINGS

Becker, W. C. *Parents are teachers: A child management program.* Champaign, Ill.: Research Press, 1971.

Eyberg, S. M., & Johnson, S. M. Multiple assessment of behavior modification with families: Effects of contingency contracting and order of treated problems. *Journal of Consulting and Clinical Psychology,* 1974, *42,* 594–606.

Holland, C. J. An interview guide for behavioral counseling with parents. *Behavior Therapy,* 1970, *1,* 70–79.

Patterson, G. R. *Living with children: New methods for parents and teachers* (Rev. ed.). Champaign, Ill.: Research Press, 1976.

Peterson, D. R. Behavior problems of middle childhood. *Journal of Consulting Psychology,* 1961, *25,* 205–209.

PARENTS' AND CHILDREN'S REINFORCEMENT SURVEY SCHEDULE (P)

Name _____ Date _____

Age _____ Sex _____

Occupation (if employed) _____ Full-time _____ Part-time _____

Number of years: Married _____ Divorced _____ Separated _____

Number of children: Boys _____ Girls _____

Name of child referred to in schedule _____ Age _____ Sex _____

If divorced or separated, does this child live with you? Yes _____ No _____

If the answer is no, with whom does this child live? _____

Check the degree to which you like doing each of the following activities with your child.

1. Kissing and hugging your child

   Not at all _____ A little _____ A fair amount _____ Much _____ Very much _____

   Not done with your child _____

2. Having your child kiss and hug you

   Not at all _____ A little _____ A fair amount _____ Much _____ Very much _____

   Not done with your child _____

3. Teaching your child to do things

   Not at all _____ A little _____ A fair amount _____ Much _____ Very much _____

   Not done with your child _____

4. Participating in active sports with your child

   Not at all _____ A little _____ A fair amount _____ Much _____ Very much _____

   Not done with your child _____

5. Playing board or card games with your child

   Not at all _____ A little _____ A fair amount _____ Much _____ Very much _____

   Not done with your child _____

6. Reading a story to your child

   Not at all _____ A little _____ A fair amount _____ Much _____ Very much _____

   Not done with your child _____

7. Hearing about your child's day (at school or otherwise)

   Not at all _____ A little _____ A fair amount _____ Much _____ Very much _____

   Not done with your child _____

8. Helping your child with his or her homework

   Not at all _____ A little _____ A fair amount _____ Much _____ Very much _____

   Not done with your child _____

9. Telling your child about your day's activities

   Not at all _____ A little _____ A fair amount _____ Much _____ Very much _____

   Not done with your child _____

10. Having long talks with your child

    Not at all _____ A little _____ A fair amount _____ Much _____ Very much _____

    Not done with your child _____

11. Giving advice to your child

   Not at all _____ A little _____ A fair amount _____ Much _____ Very much _____

   Not done with your child _____

12. Talking to your child on the telephone

   Not at all _____ A little _____ A fair amount _____ Much _____ Very much _____

   Not done with your child _____

13. Going shopping with your child

   Not at all _____ A little _____ A fair amount _____ Much _____ Very much _____

   Not done with your child _____

14. Riding in a car with your child

   Not at all _____ A little _____ A fair amount _____ Much _____ Very much _____

   Not done with your child _____

15. Going for a walk with your child

   Not at all _____ A little _____ A fair amount _____ Much _____ Very much _____

   Not done with your child _____

16. Going to the movies with your child

   Not at all _____ A little _____ A fair amount _____ Much _____ Very much _____

   Not done with your child _____

17. Watching television with your child

   Not at all _____ A little _____ A fair amount _____ Much _____ Very much _____

   Not done with your child _____

18. Attending sports events with your child

   Not at all _____ A little _____ A fair amount _____ Much _____ Very much _____

   Not done with your child _____

19. Being with your child as much as possible

   Not at all _____ A little _____ A fair amount _____ Much _____ Very much _____

   Not done with your child _____

20. Going on vacation with your child

   Not at all _____ A little _____ A fair amount _____ Much _____ Very much _____

   Not done with your child _____

21. Jogging with your child

   Not at all _____ A little _____ A fair amount _____ Much _____ Very much _____

   Not done with your child _____

22. Singing with your child

   Not at all _____ A little _____ A fair amount _____ Much _____ Very much _____

   Not done with your child _____

23. Listening to music with your child

   Not at all _____ A little _____ A fair amount _____ Much _____ Very much _____

   Not done with your child _____

24. Having your child help you work around the house or yard

   Not at all _____ A little _____ A fair amount _____ Much _____ Very much _____

   Not done with your child _____

25. Going on a picnic with your child

Not at all _____ A little _____ A fair amount _____ Much _____ Very much _____

Not done with your child _____

26. Reading in the same room in which your child is reading

Not at all _____ A little _____ A fair amount _____ Much _____ Very much _____

Not done with your child _____

27. Riding bikes with your child

Not at all _____ A little _____ A fair amount _____ Much _____ Very much _____

Not done with your child _____

28. Cooking for your child

Not at all _____ A little _____ A fair amount _____ Much _____ Very much _____

Not done with your child _____

29. Watching your child play active sports

Not at all _____ A little _____ A fair amount _____ Much _____ Very much _____

Not done with your child _____

30. Giving your child presents

Not at all _____ A little _____ A fair amount _____ Much _____ Very much _____

Not done with your child _____

31. Getting presents from your child

Not at all _____ A little _____ A fair amount _____ Much _____ Very much _____

Not done with your child _____

32. Introducing your child to new people

Not at all _____ A little _____ A fair amount _____ Much _____ Very much _____

Not done with your child _____

33. Talking to your friends and family about your child

Not at all _____ A little _____ A fair amount _____ Much _____ Very much _____

Not done with your child _____

34. Please list here any other activities you can think of that you enjoy and that are related to your child.

_____

_____

_____

_____

PARENTS' AND CHILDREN'S REINFORCEMENT SURVEY SCHEDULE (C)

Name _____ Date _____

Age _____ Sex: Boy _____ Girl _____

School _____ Grade _____

Check which of the following you have: Father _____ Stepfather _____

Mother _____ Stepmother _____

Is your father living? Yes _____ No _____ Your mother? Yes _____ No _____

Do your parents live together? Yes _____ No _____

Do you live with both your parents? Yes _____ No _____

If not, who do you live with? _____

Check (or tell me) how much you like doing each of the following things with your mother and father (or just mother or father).

1. Kissing
   a. My mother
      Not at all _____ A little _____ Very much _____ Not done with my mother _____
   b. My father
      Not at all _____ A little _____ Very much _____ Not done with my father _____

2. Hugging
   a. My mother
      Not at all _____ A little _____ Very much _____ Not done with my mother _____
   b. My father
      Not at all _____ A little _____ Very much _____ Not done with my father _____

3. Being kissed by
   a. My mother
      Not at all _____ A little _____ Very much _____ Not done with my mother _____
   b. My father
      Not at all _____ A little _____ Very much _____ Not done with my father _____

4. Being hugged by
   a. My mother
      Not at all _____ A little _____ Very much _____ Not done with my mother _____
   b. My father
      Not at all _____ A little _____ Very much _____ Not done with my father _____

5. Playing ball with
   a. My mother
      Not at all _____ A little _____ Very much _____ Not done with my mother _____
   b. My father
      Not at all _____ A little _____ Very much _____ Not done with my father _____

6. Having a story told or read to me by
   a. My mother
      Not at all _____ A little _____ Very much _____ Not done with my mother _____
   b. My father
      Not at all _____ A little _____ Very much _____ Not done with my father _____

7. Talking about my day (at school or otherwise) to

   a. My mother

      Not at all _____ A little _____ Very much _____ Not done with my mother _____

   b. My father

      Not at all _____ A little _____ Very much _____ Not done with my father _____

8. Playing games with

   a. My mother

      Not at all _____ A little _____ Very much _____ Not done with my mother _____

   b. My father

      Not at all _____ A little _____ Very much _____ Not done with my father _____

9. Having long talks with

   a. My mother

      Not at all _____ A little _____ Very much _____ Not done with my mother _____

   b. My father

      Not at all _____ A little _____ Very much _____ Not done with my father _____

10. Getting help with my homework from

   a. My mother

      Not at all _____ A little _____ Very much _____ Not done with my mother _____

   b. My father

      Not at all _____ A little _____ Very much _____ Not done with my father _____

11. Going shopping with

   a. My mother

      Not at all _____ A little _____ Very much _____ Not done with my mother _____

   b. My father

      Not at all _____ A little _____ Very much _____ Not done with my father _____

12. Riding in a car with

   a. My mother

      Not at all _____ A little _____ Very much _____ Not done with my mother _____

   b. My father

      Not at all _____ A little _____ Very much _____ Not done with my father _____

13. Going for a walk with

   a. My mother

      Not at all _____ A little _____ Very much _____ Not done with my mother _____

   b. My father

      Not at all _____ A little _____ Very much _____ Not done with my father _____

14. Going to the movies with

   a. My mother

      Not at all _____ A little _____ Very much _____ Not done with my mother _____

   b. My father

      Not at all _____ A little _____ Very much _____ Not done with my father _____

15. Going on a picnic with

    a. My mother

        Not at all ———— A little ———— Very much ———— Not done with my mother ————

    b. My father

        Not at all ———— A little ———— Very much ———— Not done with my father ————

16. Going to sports events with

    a. My mother

        Not at all ———— A little ———— Very much ———— Not done with my mother ————

    b. My father

        Not at all ———— A little ———— Very much ———— Not done with my father ————

17. Working around the house or yard with

    a. My mother

        Not at all ———— A little ———— Very much ———— Not done with my mother ————

    b. My father

        Not at all ———— A little ———— Very much ———— Not done with my father ————

18. Riding bikes with

    a. My mother

        Not at all ———— A little ———— Very much ———— Not done with my mother ————

    b. My father

        Not at all ———— A little ———— Very much ———— Not done with my father ————

19. Jogging with

    a. My mother

        Not at all ———— A little ———— Very much ———— Not done with my mother ————

    b. My father

        Not at all ———— A little ———— Very much ———— Not done with my father ————

20. Singing with

    a. My mother

        Not at all ———— A little ———— Very much ———— Not done with my mother ————

    b. My father

        Not at all ———— A little ———— Very much ———— Not done with my father ————

21. Listening to music with

    a. My mother

        Not at all ———— A little ———— Very much ———— Not done with my mother ————

    b. My father

        Not at all ———— A little ———— Very much ———— Not done with my father ————

22. Watching television with

    a. My mother

        Not at all ———— A little ———— Very much ———— Not done with my mother ————

    b. My father

        Not at all ———— A little ———— Very much ———— Not done with my father ————

23. Going on vacation with

    a. My mother

       Not at all _____ A little _____ Very much _____ Not done with my mother _____

    b. My father

       Not at all _____ A little _____ Very much _____ Not done with my father _____

24. Eating

    a. My mother's cooking

       Not at all _____ A little _____ Very much _____

       I don't eat what my mother cooks (or she doesn't cook) _____

    b. My father's cooking

       Not at all _____ A little _____ Very much _____

       I don't eat what my father cooks (or he doesn't cook) _____

25. Getting presents from

    a. My mother

       Not at all _____ A little _____ Very much _____ Not done with my mother _____

    b. My father

       Not at all _____ A little _____ Very much _____ Not done with my father _____

26. Giving presents to

    a. My mother

       Not at all _____ A little _____ Very much _____ Not done with my mother _____

    b. My father

       Not at all _____ A little _____ Very much _____ Not done with my father _____

27. Please write any other things you enjoy doing with your mother or father. _____

_____

_____

_____

_____

PARENTS' AND CHILDREN'S REINFORCEMENT SURVEY SCHEDULE (A)

Name _____ Date _____

Age _____ Sex _____

School (if in school) _____ Grade _____

Occupation (if employed) _____

Check which of the following you have: Father _____ Stepfather _____

  Mother _____ Stepmother _____

Is your father living? Yes _____ No _____ Your mother? Yes _____ No _____

Do your parents live together? Yes _____ No _____

Do you live with both your parents? Yes _____ No _____

If not, who do you live with? _____

Check how much you like doing each of the following things with your mother and father (or just mother or father).

1. Expressing affection to

   a. Your mother

      Not at all _____ A little _____ A fair amount _____ Much _____

      Very much _____ Not done with your mother _____

   b. Your father

      Not at all _____ A little _____ A fair amount _____ Much _____

      Very much _____ Not done with your father _____

2. Having affection expressed to you by

   a. Your mother

      Not at all _____ A little _____ A fair amount _____ Much _____

      Very much _____ Not done with your mother _____

   b. Your father

      Not at all _____ A little _____ A fair amount _____ Much _____

      Very much _____ Not done with your father _____

3. Playing ball with

   a. Your mother

      Not at all _____ A little _____ A fair amount _____ Much _____

      Very much _____ Not done with your mother _____

   b. Your father

      Not at all _____ A little _____ A fair amount _____ Much _____

      Very much _____ Not done with your father _____

4. Talking about your day to

   a. Your mother

      Not at all _____ A little _____ A fair amount _____ Much _____

      Very much _____ Not done with your mother _____

   b. Your father

      Not at all _____ A little _____ A fair amount _____ Much _____

      Very much _____ Not done with your father _____

5. Playing games with

   a. Your mother

   Not at all _____ A little _____ A fair amount _____ Much _____

   Very much _____ Not done with your mother _____

   b. Your father

   Not at all _____ A little _____ A fair amount _____ Much _____

   Very much _____ Not done with your father _____

6. Having long talks with

   a. Your mother

   Not at all _____ A little _____ A fair amount _____ Much _____

   Very much _____ Not done with your mother _____

   b. Your father

   Not at all _____ A little _____ A fair amount _____ Much _____

   Very much _____ Not done with your father _____

7. Getting help with your homework from

   a. Your mother

   Not at all _____ A little _____ A fair amount _____ Much _____

   Very much _____ Not done with your mother _____

   b. Your father

   Not at all _____ A little _____ A fair amount _____ Much _____

   Very much _____ Not done with your father _____

8. Talking on the telephone with

   a. Your mother

   Not at all _____ A little _____ A fair amount _____ Much _____

   Very much _____ Not done with your mother _____

   b. Your father

   Not at all _____ A little _____ A fair amount _____ Much _____

   Very much _____ Not done with your father _____

9. Hearing about the day from

   a. Your mother

   Not at all _____ A little _____ A fair amount _____ Much _____

   Very much _____ Not done with your mother _____

   b. Your father

   Not at all _____ A little _____ A fair amount _____ Much _____

   Very much _____ Not done with your father _____

10. Going shopping with

   a. Your mother

   Not at all _____ A little _____ A fair amount _____ Much _____

   Very much _____ Not done with your mother _____

   b. Your father

   Not at all _____ A little _____ A fair amount _____ Much _____

   Very much _____ Not done with your father _____

11. Riding in a car with

   a. Your mother

      Not at all _____ A little _____ A fair amount _____ Much _____

      Very much _____ Not done with your mother _____

   b. Your father

      Not at all _____ A little _____ A fair amount _____ Much _____

      Very much _____ Not done with your father _____

12. Going for a walk with

   a. Your mother

      Not at all _____ A little _____ A fair amount _____ Much _____

      Very much _____ Not done with your mother _____

   b. Your father

      Not at all _____ A little _____ A fair amount _____ Much _____

      Very much _____ Not done with your father _____

13. Going to the movies with

   a. Your mother

      Not at all _____ A little _____ A fair amount _____ Much _____

      Very much _____ Not done with your mother _____

   b. Your father

      Not at all _____ A little _____ A fair amount _____ Much _____

      Very much _____ Not done with your father _____

14. Going on a picnic with

   a. Your mother

      Not at all _____ A little _____ A fair amount _____ Much _____

      Very much _____ Not done with your mother _____

   b. Your father

      Not at all _____ A little _____ A fair amount _____ Much _____

      Very much _____ Not done with your father _____

15. Reading in the same room in which

   a. Your mother is reading

      Not at all _____ A little _____ A fair amount _____ Much _____

      Very much _____ Not done with your mother _____

   b. Your father is reading

      Not at all _____ A little _____ A fair amount _____ Much _____

      Very much _____ Not done with your father _____

16. Going to sports events with

   a. Your mother

      Not at all _____ A little _____ A fair amount _____ Much _____

      Very much _____ Not done with your mother _____

   b. Your father

      Not at all _____ A little _____ A fair amount _____ Much _____

      Very much _____ Not done with your father _____

17. Working around the house or yard with

    a. Your mother

        Not at all _____ A little _____ A fair amount _____ Much _____

        Very much _____ Not done with your mother _____

    b. Your father

        Not at all _____ A little _____ A fair amount _____ Much _____

        Very much _____ Not done with your father _____

18. Riding bikes with

    a. Your mother

        Not at all _____ A little _____ A fair amount _____ Much _____

        Very much _____ Not done with your mother _____

    b. Your father

        Not at all _____ A little _____ A fair amount _____ Much _____

        Very much _____ Not done with your father _____

19. Jogging with

    a. Your mother

        Not at all _____ A little _____ A fair amount _____ Much _____

        Very much _____ Not done with your mother _____

    b. Your father

        Not at all _____ A little _____ A fair amount _____ Much _____

        Very much _____ Not done with your father _____

20. Singing with

    a. Your mother

        Not at all _____ A little _____ A fair amount _____ Much _____

        Very much _____ Not done with your mother _____

    b. Your father

        Not at all _____ A little _____ A fair amount _____ Much _____

        Very much _____ Not done with your father _____

21. Listening to music with

    a. Your mother

        Not at all _____ A little _____ A fair amount _____ Much _____

        Very much _____ Not done with your mother _____

    b. Your father

        Not at all _____ A little _____ A fair amount _____ Much _____

        Very much _____ Not done with your father _____

22. Watching television with

    a. Your mother

        Not at all _____ A little _____ A fair amount _____ Much _____

        Very much _____ Not done with your mother _____

    b. Your father

        Not at all _____ A little _____ A fair amount _____ Much _____

        Very much _____ Not done with your father _____

23. Going on vacation with

    a. Your mother

      Not at all _____ A little _____ A fair amount _____ Much _____

      Very much _____ Not done with your mother _____

    b. Your father

      Not at all _____ A little _____ A fair amount _____ Much _____

      Very much _____ Not done with your father _____

24. Eating

    a. Your mother's cooking

      Not at all _____ A little _____ A fair amount _____ Much _____

      Very much _____ You don't eat what your mother cooks (or she doesn't cook) _____

    b. Your father's cooking

      Not at all _____ A little _____ A fair amount _____ Much _____

      Very much _____ You don't eat what your father cooks (or he doesn't cook) _____

25. Getting presents from

    a. Your mother

      Not at all _____ A little _____ A fair amount _____ Much _____

      Very much _____ Not done with your mother _____

    b. Your father

      Not at all _____ A little _____ A fair amount _____ Much _____

      Very much _____ Not done with your father _____

26. Giving presents to

    a. Your mother

      Not at all _____ A little _____ A fair amount _____ Much _____

      Very much _____ Not done with your mother _____

    b. Your father

      Not at all _____ A little _____ A fair amount _____ Much _____

      Very much _____ Not done with your father _____

27. Introducing to your friends

    a. Your mother

      Not at all _____ A little _____ A fair amount _____ Much _____

      Very much _____ Not done with your mother _____

    b. Your father

      Not at all _____ A little _____ A fair amount _____ Much _____

      Very much _____ Not done with your father _____

28. Please write any other things you enjoy doing with your mother or father. _____

_____

_____

_____

_____

_____

_____

REINFORCEMENT MENU (C and A)

RATIONALE/PURPOSE

In the treatment of many maladaptive behaviors it is often helpful to have ready a number of alternate activities available to the client to be performed in place of the undesirable behavior. For example, a client being treated for overeating may become aware of a powerful urge to eat. After using thought-stopping, relaxation, and pleasant imagery to help stop the urge, it is very effective if he can immediately turn to an alternate reinforcing activity to replace the enjoyment lost by not eating. Similarly, in teaching other clients to control physical pain responses, this list of immediately available sources of reinforcement aids in distraction from pain and in extinguishing the attention usually given to the pain experience. For these reasons, the Reinforcement Menu was developed.

ADMINISTRATION

Form A can be given to adolescents to fill out at a convenient time. Form C can be administered with the help of the parent, guardian, or therapist.

GUIDELINES

1. It is important to explain to the client that the items on the Reinforcement Menu are things or experiences usually available to them at a moment's notice. Winning a vacation to Walt Disney World would probably be very enjoyable (reinforcing) for a young client, but it is a very unlikely event, and as such has no place on the Reinforcement Menu.
2. The clients should be encouraged to add to the list any activities that they enjoy and that might be special to them (always keeping in mind immediate or near-immediate availability). Thus, "work on my car" might be a personal reinforcement added to the list by an adolescent who likes mechanics and who does indeed own a car in need of work.

ITEM BREAKDOWN

FORM C

Number of questions: 40

Questions	Topic
1–27, 29, 30, 33, 34	Activities the client can do alone
28, 31, 32, 35, 36	Activities the client can do with other people
37–40	Other activities

FORM A

Number of questions: 37

Questions	Topic
1–19, 24, 25, 28, 30–33	Activities the client can do alone
20–23, 26, 27, 29	Activities the client can do with other people
34–37	Other activities

USE OF THE INFORMATION

When a client has circled all the items he would enjoy doing, some discussion should follow on the availability of each reinforcing activity. Care was taken to include only items that should generally be available to most clients, but individual circumstances may vary. If after discussion it is found that any circled items are not immediately available, for one reason or another, these items should be crossed off the list.

Once availability has been established, the therapist, with the help of the client, should prioritize the circled items, with the first being the most enjoyable. The client may then be directed to use a reinforcing activity as an alternative to an unwanted behavior every time the need arises during the coming weeks. Feedback on how reinforcing and distracting the activity actually was can be gained in later therapeutic sessions.

It should be suggested to the client that he choose one or a couple of reinforcing activities from the menu in the morning, in order to be prepared for on-the-spot need. If, for example, a young client begins to bite his fingernails, he won't have to scan the list to find an alternate adaptive activity. Having already chosen an activity such as riding a bicycle, he can walk toward the bike immediately upon realizing that he is biting his fingernails.

The therapist is cautioned to guard against satiation in using these reinforcers. Thus, the client should be encouraged to choose different reinforcers at least every few days, if not each day.

COMPARISON TO OTHER FORMS

BEHAVIORAL RATING CARD: When using the Behavioral Rating Card, the client often is helped to achieve the designated goals by having readily available alternatives that compete with the behaviors that are to be eliminated. The Reinforcement Menu is helpful in providing these alternatives.

MOTIVATION ASSESSMENT OF PARENTS AND CHILDREN: If motivation is assessed as being low, the therapist should review all the reinforcement survey schedules and the Reinforcement Menu. Perhaps the rewards being used currently are not appropriate enough to motivate the client at a certain point in treatment.

PARENTS' AND CHILDREN'S REINFORCEMENT SURVEY SCHEDULE: Reinforcing activities that parents and children perform together may also fulfill the criterion of immediate availability and be used in the Reinforcement Menu.

REINFORCEMENT SURVEY SCHEDULES: These are more general lists of what may be reinforcing to the young client. All the items on these larger lists may not necessarily be immediately available, but those that are would be very reinforcing. Highly rated items on the Reinforcement Survey Schedules may be the basis for therapy involving positive imagery, but it remains for the Reinforcement Menu to present a list of reinforcing behaviors in which a client can actually engage at almost any time.

SCHOOL REINFORCEMENT SURVEY SCHEDULE: Pleasant school experiences may fulfill the criterion of immediate availability to the client and be used in the Reinforcement Menu.

RECOMMENDED READINGS

Ayllon, T., & Azrin, N. *The token economy: A motivational system for therapy and rehabilitation.* New York: Appleton-Century-Crofts, 1968.

Cautela, J. R. Covert reinforcement. *Behavior Therapy,* 1970, *1,* 33–50.

Cautela, J. R. Reinforcement survey schedule: Evaluation and current applications. *Psychological Reports,* 1972, *30,* 683–690.

Cautela, J. R., & Brion-Meisels, L. A children's reinforcement survey schedule. *Psychological Reports,* 1979, *44,* 327–338.

Cautela, J. R., & Kastenbaum, R. A reinforcement survey schedule for use in therapy, training, and research. *Psychological Reports,* 1967, *20,* 1115–1130.

Cautela, J. R., & Wisocki, P. The use of the reinforcement survey schedule in behavior therapy. In R. D. Rubin, H. Fensterheim, A. A. Lazarus, & C. M. Franks (Eds.), *Advances in behavior therapy: Proceedings of the third conference of the Association for Advancement of Behavior Therapy.* New York: Academic Press, 1971.

Daley, M. F. The "reinforcement menu": Finding effective reinforcers. In E. J. Mash & L. G. Terdal (Eds.), *Behavior therapy assessment: Diagnosis, design and evaluation.* New York: Springer, 1976.

REINFORCEMENT MENU (C)

Name _____ Date _____

Age _____ Sex: Boy _____ Girl _____

School _____ Grade _____

Below are activities you could do when you are bored or instead of something you are not supposed to do. Circle the ones you would enjoy doing. On the empty lines at the end of the list, fill in anything you like to do that isn't already on the list.

1. Listening to the radio	21. Writing a letter
2. Listening to the stereo	22. Building something
3. Watching television	23. Making pudding or Jell-O
4. Riding a bicycle	24. Painting
5. Going for a walk	25. Playing with jacks
6. Shooting baskets	26. Jumping rope
7. Ice skating	27. Doing a crossword puzzle
8. Playing a game by myself	28. Helping the teacher
9. Reading a book	29. Playing with cars
10. Going to the store	30. Playing with toy people
11. Working on a hobby	31. Going to a friend's house
12. Riding on my skateboard	32. Talking on the phone
13. Jogging	33. Playing in the sandbox
14. Playing dolls	34. Playing in the bathtub
15. Playing school	35. Playing cards with someone
16. Coloring	36. Helping mom or dad
17. Drawing pictures	37. _____
18. Playing with clay	38. _____
19. Cooking	39. _____
20. Baking cookies	40. _____

REINFORCEMENT MENU (A)

Name _____ Date _____

Age _____ Sex _____

School (if in school) _____ Grade _____

Occupation (if employed) _____

Below are activities you could do when you are bored or instead of something you really shouldn't do. Circle the ones you would enjoy doing. In the empty blanks at the end of the list, fill in anything you like to do that isn't already on the list.

1. Listening to the radio
2. Listening to the stereo
3. Watching television
4. Riding a bicycle
5. Going for a walk
6. Shooting baskets
7. Ice skating
8. Playing a game by yourself
9. Reading a book
10. Going shopping
11. Working on a hobby
12. Riding on your skateboard
13. Jogging
14. Drawing pictures
15. Cooking
16. Baking
17. Writing a letter
18. Painting
19. Doing a crossword puzzle
20. Helping a teacher
21. Talking to a teacher
22. Going to a friend's house
23. Talking on the phone
24. Taking a shower
25. Taking a bath
26. Helping your mother or father
27. Talking to your mother or father
28. Playing cards alone
29. Playing cards with someone
30. Doing a puzzle
31. Building a model
32. Driving a car
33. Playing an instrument
34. _____
35. _____
36. _____
37. _____

RATIONALE/PURPOSE

In its general use the term *punishment* can be defined as the application of an aversive consequence to an undesirable behavior for the purpose of reducing or eliminating the behavior. In behavior therapy the aversive consequence is only considered a punishment *if* the behavior is reduced or eliminated. Thus, the results of the procedure indicate to the behavior therapist if the process of punishment has occurred and if the aversive consequence is in fact aversive to the person whose behavior has been targeted for change.

The business of assessing what consequences will reduce the frequency of a given behavior is at best a tough one. The therapist can become aware of possible aversive events by observing the child, by asking the parents or significant others what might be punitive to the child, or by asking the child what is punitive. In the Response Cost Survey Schedule the child or adolescent is asked to note first which items it would bother her to lose, and second which tasks it would bother her to be assigned.

Response cost is a specific type of punishment. The loss of a reinforcer or the loss of free time by being assigned a task is a situation which has had nothing to do with the maintenance of the behavior in the past. For example, a youngster who doesn't arrive home on time for dinner may find her response cost to be the loss of the opportunity to go to the school dance on Saturday or an assignment to kitchen cleanup. Neither kitchen cleanup nor missing the school dance is directly related to the behavior of being late for dinner.

ADMINISTRATION

This schedule is administered by the therapist. The child or adolescent fills it out in his presence and can ask questions at any time.

GUIDELINES

1. It may be that some youngsters, particularly adolescents, will show resistance to admitting what is personally aversive. Including the youngster in the planning of treatment sometimes reduces this resistance.
2. For some of the items, it may be helpful to discuss with the child how much time lost would bother her. For example, if the youngster is penalized for not cleaning her room, she may lose 1 hour of television watching on that particular day. One hour may or may not be long enough to be aversive.
3. In the adolescent inventory only one item suggested involves the loss of time with a parent. At this stage the activities shared between a parent and an adolescent son or daughter are generally at a minimum in frequency and duration. It may not be in the best interest of the relationship to decrease this involvement in a punitive way.

ITEM BREAKDOWN

FORM C
Number of questions: 38

Questions	Topic
1, 2, 11, 12, 20, 21, 23	Objects
14–16, 18, 19*	Activities with parents
13, 17, 19*	Activities with peers

Questions	Topic
3–10, 22	Personal time
24–27, 29–32, 34–36	Inside work
28, 33, 37	Outside work
38	Other response cost possibilities

FORM A

Number of questions: 38

Questions	Topic
1, 2, 4, 8–11, 16–18	Objects
20	Activities with parents
12, 14, 15	Activities with peers
3, 19	Personal time
5–7, 13, 21, 22	Privileges
23–27, 29, 31–37	Inside work
28, 30	Outside work
38	Other response cost possibilities

*This indicates that the item is under more than one category.

USE OF THE INFORMATION

The Response Cost Survey Schedule is a way to identify those events that are punishing to a particular child or adolescent. An attempt was made to cover a variety of settings and situations in which response cost might be utilized. Those situations that appear in the *Very much* category should be listed and, if possible, ranked in some order of magnitude. These punitive events, like rewards, should be varied so that their effectiveness is not diminished.

When a child loses a reinforcer or is assigned an aversive task, the limits of the punitive situation should be specified. Also, as with the use of any aversive technique, positive procedures should be occurring concomitantly. For example, if the child loses her allowance for not doing a given amount of homework, then a positive consequence should occur if the appropriate amount of homework is done by the child.

The response cost items also work well for the covert procedures of negative reinforcement and covert sensitization. (Covert sensitization is rarely used with children.)

COMPARISON TO OTHER FORMS

BEHAVIOR STATUS CHECKLIST and SCHOOL BEHAVIOR STATUS CHECKLIST: Once the behaviors to be targeted for change have been determined through these checklists, the response cost items may suggest consequences for certain undesirable behaviors.

GUIDELINES FOR PARENTAL DISCIPLINE: The technique of response cost is often helpful to parents needing guidance in appropriate methods of discipline.

PROGRESS CHART: In establishing a contractual agreement with a child or adolescent, it may be important to introduce response cost items as consequences for given behaviors.

RECOMMENDED READINGS

Cautela, J. R. Covert sensitization. *Psychological Reports,* 1967, *20,* 459–468.

Cautela, J. R. Covert negative reinforcement. *Journal of Behavior Therapy and Experimental Psychiatry,* 1970, *1,* 273–278.

Cautela, J. R. Covert response cost. *Psychotherapy: Theory, Research and Practice,* 1976, *13,* 397–404.

Kazdin, A. E. Response cost: The removal of conditioned reinforcers for therapeutic change. *Behavior Therapy,* 1972, *3,* 533–546.

Kazdin, A. E. *Behavior modification in applied settings* (Rev. ed.). Homewood, Ill.: Dorsey Press, 1980.

Rimm, D. C., & Masters, J. C. *Behavior therapy: Techniques and empirical findings.* New York: Academic Press, 1974.

RESPONSE COST SURVEY SCHEDULE (C)

Name _____ Date _____

Age _____ Sex: Boy _____ Girl _____

School _____ Grade _____

How much would it bother you to *lose* the following things or privileges? Put an X in the box that tells best how you would feel.

	Not at all	A little	Very much
1. A favorite toy			
2. My allowance			
3. The chance to watch my favorite television program			
4. The chance to watch television for the evening			
5. Playtime after school			
6. Playtime on Saturday			
7. Playtime after dinner			
8. Playtime on Sunday			
9. Playtime in my room			
10. The chance to stay up until my regular bedtime			
11. Dessert			
12. My snack			
13. Going to a friend's house			
14. Going out for a treat such as ice cream with my parents			
15. Going out to eat with my parents			
16. Going to the movies with my parents			
17. Going to the movies with a friend			
18. Going to the zoo with my parents			
19. Going to a			
a. football game			
b. basketball game			
c. hockey game			
d. baseball game			
e. soccer game			
20. My bicycle			
21. My favorite game			
22. The chance to watch cartoons on Saturday morning			
23. Money			
a. 5 cents			
b. 10 cents			
c. 25 cents			
d. 1 dollar			
e. 5 dollars			

How much would it bother you to be assigned the following jobs? Put an X in the box that tells best how you would feel.

	Not at all	A little	Very much
24. Washing the dishes			
25. Vacuuming			
26. Dusting the furniture			
27. Changing the sheets on my bed			
28. Cleaning the inside of the car			
29. Washing the windows			
30. Washing the kitchen floor			
31. Cleaning the bathroom			
32. Washing the floor			
33. Raking leaves			
34. Taking the garbage out			
35. Drying dishes			
36. Cleaning my room			
37. Weeding the garden			

38. Please write down (or tell me) other things or privileges you would not like to lose or jobs you would not want to be given. _____

_____

_____

_____

_____

RESPONSE COST SURVEY SCHEDULE (A)

Name _____ Date _____

Age _____ Sex _____

School (if in school) _____ Grade _____

Occupation (if employed) _____

How much would it bother you to *lose* the following items or privileges? Put a check mark in the column that best describes how you would feel.

	Not at all	A little	Very much
1. Access to the car			
2. Your allowance			
3. The privilege of watching television			
4. Your bicycle			
5. Phone privileges			
6. The chance to earn money			
7. The privilege of going out after school			
8. Access to the stereo			
9. Access to the radio or tape recorder			
10. Access to your blow dryer			
11. Access to the sewing machine or tools			
12. A chance to go to			
a. a school dance			
b. a football game			
c. a basketball game			
d. a baseball game			
e. a hockey game			
f. after-school activities			
13. A chance to go shopping			
14. Time with a friend			
15. A chance to spend the night with a friend			
16. Your favorite shoes			
17. Your favorite sweater or blouse			
18. Your wallet or purse			
19. Time to work on a craft or hobby			
20. Time with your mother or father			
21. The privilege of going out			
a. Saturday night			
b. Friday night			
c. Saturday during the day			
d. Sunday during the day			
22. The chance to play in a sports event			

How much would it bother you to be assigned the following jobs? Put a check mark in the column that best describes how you would feel.

	Not at all	A little	Very much
23. Cleaning the bathroom			
24. Cleaning the garage			
25. Cleaning the basement			
26. Cleaning the attic			
27. Washing windows			
28. Washing the car			
29. Cleaning your room			
30. Mowing the lawn			
31. Washing your clothes			
32. Washing the clothes of all family members			
33. Vacuuming several rooms			
34. Dusting the furniture in several rooms			
35. Washing the dishes			
36. Cooking dinner			
37. Washing the kitchen floor			

38. Please write down other things or privileges you would not like to lose or jobs you would not want to be assigned. _____

_____

_____

_____

_____

_____

SCHOOL REINFORCEMENT SURVEY SCHEDULE (C and A)

RATIONALE/PURPOSE

The School Reinforcement Survey Schedule was developed to determine to what degree a student finds attending class, doing homework, and socializing with school friends reinforcing.

ADMINISTRATION

Most adolescents should be able to complete this form on their own. Some adolescents and most children will need to have the therapist present to clarify some items.

GUIDELINES

1. Some of the items on the School Reinforcement Survey Schedule isolate one small event in the response chain of behaviors leading up to attending school, e.g., Question 3, "Entering the school building." It may be that some students have never stopped to evaluate their feelings about such a particular action. For such students it is often helpful to have them close their eyes and imagine they are entering their particular school building in the morning and then describe their feelings upon doing so.

2. Question 19 on Form C and Question 21 on Form A list three school vacation times together. If a student wishes to differentiate feelings of anticipation for school after each of the three separate vacations listed, the information is apt to be helpful. This item was constructed as one idea because of the brevity of these holidays in contrast to the extended summer vacation and because all school systems don't give the same seasonal vacations.

3. Unlike the 5-point rating system on Form A, Form C has only a 3-point rating system. This shorter system is meant to make it easy for the younger client to rate degree of reinforcement.

ITEM BREAKDOWN

FORM C

Number of questions: 31

Questions	Topic
1–4	Going to school
5–7	Participating in free-time activities
8, 9	Doing schoolwork
10–13	Talking about school to others
14, 15	Seeing the report card
16, 17	Participating in extracurricular activities
18–20	Looking forward to school after breaks
21–30	Learning subjects
31	Having enjoyable experiences in school

FORM A

Number of questions: 37

Questions	Topic
1–4	Going to school
5–7	Participating in free-time activities
8–10	Doing schoolwork
11–14	Talking about school to others
15, 16	Seeing the report card
17–21	Participating in extracurricular activities
22–24	Looking forward to school after breaks
25–36	Learning subjects
37	Having enjoyable experiences in school

USE OF THE INFORMATION

The School Reinforcement Survey Schedule can be utilized to discover what aspects of school attendance a student finds reinforcing. The student can then be taught to focus upon the reinforcing aspects of school and perhaps begin to spend more time participating in these activities. If, for example, an individual finds school generally aversive, he may be asked to complete this schedule and thus become aware of those aspects of school that *are* enjoyable to him. The client then can learn to focus on and improve upon these reinforcing aspects, possibly making the general school experience more rewarding. This may lead to increased school attendance.

In the treatment phase of therapy, some of the reinforcing items from the School Reinforcement Survey Schedule can be utilized as rewards to increase the frequency of behaviors that need to be increased or as response costs when inappropriate behaviors are emitted. Further, this form can be used in the behavioral analysis of school phobias.

COMPARISON TO OTHER FORMS

BEHAVIORAL RATING CARD: This card lists certain target behaviors; for short-term rewards for this program, the School Reinforcement Survey Schedule would be an excellent source.

PARENTS' AND CHILDREN'S REINFORCEMENT SURVEY SCHEDULE: This more general reinforcement form should give a comprehensive indication of what may be reinforcing to the client. It should also relate to some of the parent-child items on the School Reinforcement Survey Schedule.

REINFORCEMENT MENU: For the full-time student, pleasant school experiences may fulfill the criterion of immediate availability necessary for inclusion on the Reinforcement Menu.

REINFORCEMENT SURVEY SCHEDULES: There is often overlapping information in these more general reinforcement scales and the scales assessing reinforcement in particular settings (as this school schedule).

SCHOOL BEHAVIOR STATUS CHECKLIST: Once the therapist has determined the school behaviors to be targeted for change, the next step is to find possible reinforcers within the school environment.

RECOMMENDED READINGS

Homme, L., Csanyi, A. P., Gonzales, M. A., & Rechs, J. R. *How to use contingency contracting in the classroom.* Champaign, Ill.: Research Press, 1970.

Kazdin, A. E. *Behavior modification in applied settings* (Rev. ed.). Homewood, Ill.: Dorsey Press, 1980.

SCHOOL REINFORCEMENT SURVEY SCHEDULE (C)

Name _____ Date _____

Age _____ Sex: Boy _____ Girl _____

School _____ Grade _____

Put an X in the box that tells best how much you like each of these things about school.

	Not at all	A little	Very much
1. Leaving my home for school in the morning			
2. Riding or walking to school			
3. Going into the school building			
4. Going into my classroom and talking to my teacher alone			
5. Having recess			
6. Having lunch with the other children			
7. Playing with the other children			
8. Working with the other children in groups in my classroom			
9. Doing my homework			
10. Talking about school with my mother			
11. Talking about school with my father			
12. Talking about school with my friends after school			
13. Telling children who don't go to my school all about my school			
14. Seeing my report card			
15. Having my parents see my report card			
16. Being in or going to school sports events			
17. Going to special events like class trips, fairs, or school plays			
18. Being glad to go back to school at the end of summer vacation			
19. Being glad to go back to school at the end of Christmas, mid-winter, and spring vacations			
20. Being glad to go back to school each Monday morning after the weekend			

Put an X in the box that tells best how much you like learning each of the following things.

	Not at all	A little	Very much	Do not learn that
21. Reading				
22. Language arts				
23. Math				
24. A foreign language				
25. Social studies				
26. Art				
27. Music				
28. Science				
29. Gym				
30. Religion				

31. Tell about the three things that happen in school that you like most:

    1. _____

    2. _____

    3. _____

SCHOOL REINFORCEMENT SURVEY SCHEDULE (A)

Name _____ Date _____

Age _____ Sex _____

School _____ Grade _____

Put a check mark in the column that best describes how much you like each of the following school-related activities.

	Not at all	A little	A fair amount	Much	Very much
1. Leaving your home for school in the morning					
2. Riding or walking to school					
3. Entering the school building					
4. Entering your home classroom and talking to your teacher alone					
5. Having recess or free time					
6. Having lunch with the other students					
7. Playing or socializing with the other students (sports, etc.)					
8. Doing classroom activities					
9. Studying with the other students in the study hall					
10. Doing your homework					
11. Talking about school with your mother					
12. Talking about school with your father					
13. Talking about school with your friends after school					
14. Talking about your school with friends who attend a different school					
15. Seeing your report card					
16. Having your parents see your report card					
17. Going to school sports events					
18. Going to school dances or fairs					
19. Going to after-school clubs and meetings					
20. Going to school plays					
21. Going on class trips					
22. Looking forward to going back to school at the end of summer vacation					

	Not at all	A little	A fair amount	Much	Very much
23. Looking forward to going back to school at the end of the Christmas, mid-winter, and spring vacations					
24. Looking forward to going back to school each Monday morning after the weekend					

Put a check mark in the column that best describes how much you like learning each of the following subjects.

	Not at all	A little	A fair amount	Much	Very much	Do not take
25. English						
26. Math						
27. A foreign language						
28. Social studies						
29. History						
30. Art						
31. Music						
32. Science						
33. Industrial arts						
34. Physical education (gym)						
35. Religion						
36. Reading (literature)						

37. Name the three things that happen in school that you like most:

    1. _____

    2. _____

    3. _____

Recording Baseline Data

BEHAVIOR RECORD FORM (P, T, or S)

RATIONALE/PURPOSE

The Behavior Record Form provides the observer of the child, be it parent, teacher, principal, or therapist, with an organized method for recording the important components of the target behavior. The form is useful in both the preprogram or baseline phase and in the treatment or intervention phase. Once the target behavior has been clearly and functionally defined, the observer will need to record data on the behavior in terms of a behavioral analysis commonly referred to as the ABC paradigm (antecedent, behavior, consequence). The areas most often addressed in the behavioral analysis are:

Frequency: The number of times a behavior occurs within a specified time period

Intensity: The strength of the behavior per occurrence on a scale of 1 to 5; the key for intensity is at the top of the page

Duration: The length of each episode of the behavior

Antecedents: Events prior to the behavior that may be cuing the behavior

Consequences: Events occurring after the behavior that may be maintaining the behavior

ADMINISTRATION

Someone skilled in behavioral techniques should oversee the use of this form. The observation can be done by a parent, a member of the school staff, a therapist, or a party unrelated to the situation. The information gathered should be reviewed on a frequent basis.

GUIDELINES

1. If a person other than the parent or guardian is observing the child, permission from the parent or guardian for the observation is necessary.
2. The target behavior should be defined in such a way that two or more observers would be able to reliably record it. A reliability check is an important facet of any behavioral program.
3. For the inexperienced recorder (for example, a parent), the chosen methods of collecting data should be explained at length. The recorder should be apprised of helpful tools in measurement such as the wrist counter and stopwatch.
4. Baseline data should be taken for at least 1 week. In the school system a school week will generally be sufficient.
5. Look at the Sample Behavior Record Form on page 157.
    a. The child's name, dates covered by the form, and the name of the person recording and his or her relationship to the child are to be filled in on the top lines.
    b. In the space labeled *Target behavior,* a phrase describing the target behavior in measurable terms should be inserted.
    c. The phase to which the observation applies should be circled.
    d. For each occurrence of a behavior, one or more of the following measurements can be recorded: frequency, intensity, and duration. The therapist should determine which measurements should be taken before recording begins.

    In the *Frequency* column, a check should be placed each time a behavior occurs. In the *Intensity* column, a number from 1 to 5 is recorded based on the intensity key at the top of the page. The therapist and the person who will record should review criteria for intensity levels so that a number can be assigned to the level of behavior with some reliability. Finally, in the *Duration* column, the length of time over which the behavior occurs is recorded.
    e. The events occurring before and after the target behavior are to be noted in the *Antecedents* and *Consequences* columns. Examples of possible antecedents and consequences should be reviewed by the therapist and the person who will be recording.

f. All information should be written down as close in time to the event as is practical.

g. If a behavior occurs very frequently and more space is needed for recording, a blank sheet may be attached to the form for writing down the additional information.

6. In the cases of fear, anxiety, or pain behavior, the measurements of intensity and duration of response usually indicate the amount of behavior change more clearly than frequency. The frequency of the fear, anxiety, and pain stimuli is not under the control of those working to change the behavior.

7. It is often helpful to graph the information accumulated from the Behavior Record Form. A visual representation can be very encouraging to those involved in the program.

8. The Behavior Record Form should not be seen during the baseline phase by the child being observed.

USE OF THE INFORMATION

Baseline data should be used as a basis for formulating the treatment program. Occasionally it becomes clear from the baseline data that the wrong behavior is being targeted; at this point the parties involved should reconsider which behavior(s) in fact needs remediation.

To the person skilled in behavioral techniques, the behavioral analysis should provide enough information to establish a course of action. It goes beyond the scope of this manual to instruct the reader in behavioral methodology. Some of the sources in the Recommended Readings section may be helpful for those in search of appropriate methods for specific problems.

COMPARISON TO OTHER FORMS

BEHAVIORAL RATING CARD: The Behavior Record Form gives an idea of the specifics of behavior in the baseline phase. Once baseline data have been considered, it may be important to include the child directly in the behavior change process by using the Behavioral Rating Card.

BEHAVIOR STATUS CHECKLIST and SCHOOL BEHAVIOR STATUS CHECKLIST: These checklists suggest to the therapist which behaviors warrant observation; the Behavior Record Form provides a form on which to record the observation.

BODILY CUES FOR TENSION AND ANXIETY: Once bodily areas of tension have been identified through this form, the Behavior Record Form can be used to discover environmental components contributing to tension.

GUIDELINES FOR TIME-OUT: Time-out may be one of the procedures chosen once the baseline data have been gathered.

HOME VISIT OBSERVATION FORM: When doing an observation in the home, it may be advantageous to use the Behavior Record Form in conjunction with the Home Visit Observation Form. The Home Visit Observation Form incorporates information of a general nature, while the Behavior Record Form assesses specific behaviors.

RECOMMENDED READINGS

Cautela, J. R. Behavior therapy and the need for behavioral assessment. *Psychotherapy: Theory, Research and Practice,* 1968, *5,* 175–179.

Goldfried, M. R., & Davison, G. C. *Clinical behavior therapy.* New York: Holt, Rinehart and Winston, 1976.

Hersen, M., & Bellack, A. S. (Eds.). *Behavioral assessment: A practical handbook.* Elmsford, N. Y.: Pergamon Press, 1976.

Kazdin, A. E. *Behavior modification in applied settings* (Rev. ed.). Homewood, Ill.: Dorsey Press, 1980.

Marholin II, D., & Bijou, S. Behavioral assessment: Listen when the data speak. In D. Marholin II (Ed.), *Child behavior therapy.* New York: Gardner Press, 1978.

Miller, W. H. *Systematic parent training: Procedures, cases and issues.* Champaign, Ill.: Research Press, 1975.

SAMPLE BEHAVIOR RECORD FORM (P, T, or S)

Name of child __Terry Johnson__   From __10/8__ to __10/14__

Person filling out form __Jeanne Johnson__   Relation to child __mother__

Target behavior __Crying when told no (can't do something, have something, or go somewhere)__

Circle which phase: (baseline)   intervention

Intensity Key: 1 — Not at all; 2 — A little; 3 — A fair amount; 4 — Much; 5 — Very much

Day	Frequency (# behaviors)	Intensity (1–5)	Duration (how long)	Antecedents (events prior to behavior)	Consequences (events after behavior)
Monday	✓	3	10 minutes	Terry asked for a candy bar.	I yelled at him.
Tuesday	✓	4	15 minutes	Terry wanted to watch television.	I explained that his dad wanted to watch a baseball game.
	✓	2	6 minutes	Terry asked to go to the movies.	I ignored his crying; his father spanked him.
Wednesday					
Thursday					
Friday					
Saturday					
Sunday					

BEHAVIOR RECORD FORM (P, T, or S)

Name of child _____ From _____ to _____

Person filling out form _____ Relation to child _____

Target behavior _____

Circle which phase: baseline   intervention

Intensity Key: 1 — Not at all; 2 — A little; 3 — A fair amount; 4 — Much; 5 — Very much

Day	Frequency (# behaviors)	Intensity (1–5)	Duration (how long)	Antecedents (events prior to behavior)	Consequences (events after behavior)
Monday					
Tuesday					
Wednesday					
Thursday					
Friday					
Saturday					
Sunday					

HOME VISIT OBSERVATION FORM (T)

RATIONALE/PURPOSE

Generally it is important to get to know the home environment of a child being seen in therapy. Often behaviors targeted for change in therapy or in the school need to be addressed in the home. The usual methods for determining the antecedents, behaviors, and consequences occurring in the home involve one, two, or all of the following: the therapist can ask the parent(s) to give an overview of what happens; the therapist can instruct the parent(s) to keep records of behaviors; or the therapist can visit the home for an observation.

The Home Visit Observation Form covers two of the above methods. It gives a format for asking the parents questions for the purpose of getting a general overview and it provides a structure for the direct home observation. This form has been designed to help the therapist focus on antecedents, target behaviors, and consequences, as well as to supply information that may be germane to the observation.

ADMINISTRATION

This form is generally intended for someone trained in psychology, counseling, social work, or a related area. Questions 2, 3, 4, and 5 should be addressed prior to the observation.

GUIDELINES

1. The questions should be answered during the observation or as soon after as possible.
2. The target behaviors to be listed in Question 3 should be ascertained prior to the observation. The frequency, intensity, and duration of each behavior should be determined in the session.
3. For Question 4, the parents may be asked what they think the antecedents and consequences are for the targeted behaviors. Then the therapist should record during the observation what the antecedents and consequences are for that specific time.
4. To answer Question 3, the therapist may opt to use a larger, more elaborate form such as the Behavior Record Form to increase the ease with which the observation is done.
5. All questions should be answered with as much specificity as time allows.
6. The visit should be arranged at a time when as many of the household members as possible are present.
7. One observation may not be sufficient. The first visit may only help determine what should in fact be observed.
8. During the observation the therapist should be as unobtrusive as possible. Any interaction with household members should be delayed until the termination of the observation period.
9. The observation should be long enough to allow all the questions on the form to be answered.

USE OF THE INFORMATION

After the observation is completed, the therapist should have enough information to initiate a behavioral program. The therapist should be aware of which behaviors are problematic to the child and disruptive to his interactions with the family, which behaviors are absent or minimal, which antecedents appear to be connected with which behaviors, and how behaviors are punished, rewarded, or ignored. Questions 3, 4, 7, 8, 10, 12, 13, and 19 should make the contingencies clear after the observation. Since this is only an assessment form, specific strategies for intervention are not included. However, the Recommended Readings have been compiled so that the reader will have a fairly comprehensive list of resources to refer to for developing a treatment strategy.

COMPARISON TO OTHER FORMS

BEHAVIOR ANALYSIS HISTORY QUESTIONNAIRE: Many of the questions in this form lead to information that will help the therapist in preparing for the home visit.

BEHAVIOR RECORD FORM: After the Home Visit Observation Form has been filled out, the next step may be having the parent(s) record the specifics about target behaviors. The Behavior Record Form can be used for this purpose.

BEHAVIOR STATUS CHECKLIST and SCHOOL BEHAVIOR STATUS CHECKLIST: By compiling the behaviors that the parents, school personnel, and child or adolescent have defined as problematic, the therapist will have some idea of what should be observed.

PARENTAL REACTION SURVEY SCHEDULE: This schedule is a measure of possible abuse or neglect of the child. If the therapist has some indication of a problem in this area, it may be helpful for the parents to fill it out.

PROGRESS CHART: The Progress Chart may be useful in setting up a program once an observation has been done.

RECOMMENDED READINGS

Berkowitz, B. P., & Graziano, A. M. Training parents as behavior therapists: A review. *Behaviour Research and Therapy,* 1972, *10,* 297–317.

Brockway, B. S., & Williams, W. W. Training in child management: A prevention-oriented model. In E. J. Mash, L. Hamerlynck, & L. Handy (Eds.), *Behavior modification approaches to parenting.* New York: Brunner/Mazel, 1976.

Johnson, M. R., Whitman, T. L., & Barloon-Noble, R. A home-based program for a preschool behaviorally disturbed child with parents as therapists. *Journal of Behavior Therapy and Experimental Psychiatry,* 1978, *9,* 65–70.

Miller, W. H. *Systematic parent training: Procedures, cases and issues.* Champaign, Ill.: Research Press, 1975.

Patterson, G. R. *Living with children: New methods for parents and teachers* (Rev. ed.). Champaign, Ill.: Research Press, 1976.

Weathers, L., & Liberman, R. Modification of family behavior. In D. Marholin II (Ed.), *Child behavior therapy.* New York: Gardner Press, 1978.

HOME VISIT OBSERVATION FORM (T)

Name of child _____

Name of parent or guardian _____

Date and time of visit _____ Amount of time _____

Observation made by _____ Title _____

1. List the individuals present at the time of the visit.

   _____   _____

   _____   _____

   _____   _____

   _____

2. Describe prior contact with the child and family and give information pertinent to the observation.

   _____

   _____

   _____

   _____

   _____

   _____

3. List the target behaviors being observed and indicate the measurements being used (F=frequency, I=intensity, D=duration, L=latency).

	F	I	D	L
a.				
b.				
c.				
d.				
e.				

4. List the antecedents and consequences to respective target behaviors.

   a. _____

   b. _____

   c. _____

   d. _____

   e. _____

5. List the members of the household, their ages, and their occupations.

Name	Age	Occupation

6. Describe the physical surroundings in which the child lives. Does the child share a room with someone? Does he or she keep the bedroom clean? _____

_____

_____

_____

_____

7. What ways was the child rewarded during the observation?

Behavior rewarded	Reward
_____	_____
_____	_____
_____	_____
_____	_____
_____	_____

8. What ways was the child punished?

Behavior punished	Punishment
_____	_____
_____	_____
_____	_____
_____	_____
_____	_____

9. What positive statements were made about the child to someone else (e.g., compliments, encouraging remarks, or indications of approval)?

Statement	Person who made statement
_____	_____
_____	_____
_____	_____
_____	_____
_____	_____

10. What positive statements were made to the child about the child?

Statement	Person who made statement
_____	_____
_____	_____
_____	_____
_____	_____
_____	_____

11. What negative statements were made about the child to someone else?

Statement	Person who made statement
_____	_____
_____	_____
_____	_____
_____	_____
_____	_____

12. What negative statements were made to the child about the child?

Statement	Person who made statement
_____	_____
_____	_____
_____	_____
_____	_____
_____	_____

13. Describe affectionate behavior shown to the child during the observation.

Behavior	Person displaying behavior
_____	_____
_____	_____
_____	_____
_____	_____
_____	_____

14. Describe affectionate behavior of the child toward others.

Behavior	Person to whom behavior displayed
_____	_____
_____	_____
_____	_____
_____	_____
_____	_____

15. Were there any quarrels among family members? If so, describe. _____

_____

_____

_____

_____

16. In what ways did the individuals present respond to the child's requests? _____

_____

_____

_____

_____

17. Did the child initiate helping activities? If so, describe. _____

_____

_____

_____

_____

18. Did any problems arise for any family members during the observation? If so, describe the problem(s) and the method(s) of problem solving. _____

_____

_____

_____

_____

_____

19. Were there behaviors of the child that individuals did not attend to? _____

_____

_____

_____

_____

20. What activities occurred during the observation? _____

_____

_____

_____

_____

21. Did your presence inhibit the behavior of any household member? If so, to what degree and whose behavior? _____

_____

_____

_____

_____

22. List significant maladaptive behaviors of the child that you noted. _____

_____

_____

_____

_____

23. List significant adaptive behaviors of the child that you noted. _____

_____

_____

_____

_____

24. List any other pertinent facts noted in the observation. _____

_____

_____

_____

_____

_____

Intervention Recording
and Guidelines

BEHAVIORAL RATING CARD (S)

RATIONALE/PURPOSE

The Behavioral Rating Card is a form to be used in programming behavior change for an individual within a school or institutional environment. It is a tool by which a child can receive feedback across situations, behaviors, and individuals; it is also a means by which the behaviors being targeted can be maintained and generalized, and in which the interfering effects among multiple interventions can be kept to a minimum. In schools and institutions, a collaboration of efforts is often important in order that the child or adolescent receive consistent responses for a given behavior. Such collaboration can be difficult to manage, given the diverse roles and responsibilities of teachers and other staff members. Thus, the most generally workable method is the one that is the least complicated and the most time efficient. The use of the Behavioral Rating Card provides such a method. It not only allows staff members to give the child feedback close in time to the target behaviors, but it also stresses their looking at the child's behavior in a positive way.

ADMINISTRATION

Someone skilled in behavioral techniques should oversee the use of this form. This person should review the card at least twice a week to be sure that the guidelines are being followed.

GUIDELINES

1. Possible target behaviors should be discussed by the parties involved, and then observations should be made in each of the areas in which the card will be used. The observations should disclose specifically which behaviors are problematic. The Behavior Record Form may be used during the observation phase.
2. The program should start with only two or three behaviors so that those involved in the program, including the student, don't find the task overwhelming.
3. There are two types of Behavioral Rating Cards: Type I and Type II. The Type I card is used for young children, special needs children, and students who spend most of their day with a limited number of adults. The Type II card is for older students or students who change classes.
4. Look at the Sample Type I Behavioral Rating Card on page 170.
   Front of card
   a. The student's name and the dates the card spans are to be placed on the top lines.
   b. In the *Target Behaviors* column, a phrase is to be filled in below each number to remind the student and the staff members of the specific behavior being watched. The numbers correspond to target behavior definitions on the back of the card.
   c. Points or stars are to be placed by the staff member in the appropriate box when the targeted behavior is performed.
   d. In the lower right-hand corner there are two boxes for recording points, *Points from last week* and *Total points*. The box *Points from last week* should contain the number of points from last week that were not turned in for a Big Reward. (Little Rewards do not require the student to give up any points.) *Total points* should display the total of all the current week's points plus the points from last week. This box is completed at the end of each week.
   Back of card
   e. In the numbered spaces, each target behavior should be defined so that all parties, including the student, know what particular behavior is expected and how it is measured. For example, if Sara sits in her seat for 15 minutes, sitting being when her body is firmly in the seat with her feet on the floor, she receives one star or point. All parties involved should be aware of the minimum requirements for the behavior, that is, how many, how long, or to what degree a behavior must be emitted in order to be worth a point.

f. The number of points needed for Big and Little Rewards is to be filled in at the bottom of the card. The rewards and the number of points necessary to earn them should be agreed upon by the coordinator and student before the program begins. A Little Reward generally is a small privilege, such as reading the salute to the flag over the public address system. A small number of points must be earned for such a reward. The Big Reward should be something important and large, such as a chance to go bowling with one of the staff members involved in the program. To obtain the Big Reward, the child would have to earn many points.

5. Look at the Sample Type II Behavioral Rating Card on page 172.

Front of card

a. The spaces for the student's name and the beginning and ending dates of the week are to be filled in.

b. In the *Subject Areas* column, the name of the subject corresponding to each class period in which the behavior is to be monitored is to be written in. (More subject areas may be added, if needed.)

c. The numbered rows are the places where points are filled in by the staff member for behaviors performed. Each number corresponds to a target behavior listed on the back of the card.

Back of card

d. For each numbered space, a target behavior should be operationally defined, with the means of measurement stated. Within the definition key words should be chosen and underlined as a reminder to the student and staff.

e. The space labeled *Points from last week* should show the number of points from last week not turned in for a Big Reward. (Points are not taken away when a Little Reward is given.) In the space labeled *Total points* the coordinator should fill in the total of all the points earned by the end of the week plus those carried over from last week.

f. The number of points needed to earn Big and Little Rewards are to be placed in the appropriate spaces. (See 4f for more on Big and Little Rewards.)

6. The card is to be filled in by each involved staff member in the presence of the child, as close in time to the behavior as possible. For older students it may be better to fill the card in at the end of the class period. Care should be taken not to embarrass the student when giving points. Often this can be averted by simply asking the student how she would like it done.

7. Putting the Behavioral Rating Card on a 5 × 8-inch index card works very well. It can be folded into thirds and easily placed in the student's pocket, purse, or desk, or on the teacher's desk.

8. For other than very young or special needs students, the presentation of the card can be the responsibility of the student. Thus, if the card is not presented, the student misses out on the points that may have been earned.

9. Those members of the staff who are involved should meet on a regular basis to review the efficacy of the program. A graph of the frequency of each behavior should be presented at each meeting. During these review sessions, staff members should be told of such phenomena as the extinction burst, spontaneous recovery, deprivation, and satiation. Reinforcers should be examined closely for their continued effectiveness, and staff members should be reminded of the importance of awarding points as close in time to the behavior as possible and of pairing praise with the awarding of points. The amount of prompting that is to be done should also be discussed.

USE OF THE INFORMATION

The Behavioral Rating Card serves several important purposes. First, it is a collection of data regarding specific behaviors. It is also a visual representation of the progress the child is making on each behavior. It facilitates collaboration on a program for the child, and, since it is a relatively easy method for teachers to use to reward appropriate behavior, it fosters a positive attitude toward the child.

COMPARISON TO OTHER FORMS

BEHAVIOR RECORD FORM: This recording form may be used in the observation phase.

BEHAVIOR STATUS CHECKLIST (C and A): This checklist may help identify problem behaviors. Targeting a behavior that the child wishes to change can be a positive way to involve the child in the program.

REINFORCEMENT MENU: Reinforcers listed on the Menu that are appropriate may also be used in the Behavioral Rating Card program.

REINFORCEMENT SURVEY SCHEDULES: These general reinforcement survey schedules can provide suggestions for reinforcers to be used in the Behavioral Rating Card program.

SCHOOL BEHAVIOR STATUS CHECKLIST: The checklist will help in the identification of possible target behaviors. It would be used at the onset of planning.

SCHOOL REINFORCEMENT SURVEY SCHEDULE: Data from this schedule are likely to supply some appropriate reinforcers for the Behavioral Rating Card program.

RECOMMENDED READINGS

Blanchard, E. B., & Johnson, R. A. Generalization of operant classroom control procedures. *Behavior Therapy,* 1973, *4,* 219–229.

Kazdin, A. E. *The token economy: A review and evaluation.* New York: Plenum, 1977.

Lovitt, T. C. Self-management projects with children with behavioral disabilities. *Journal of Learning Disabilities,* 1973, *6,* 138–150.

SAMPLE TYPE I
BEHAVIORAL RATING CARD (S)

FRONT OF CARD

| Name of student _Sara Evans_ | | From _10/4_ | to _10/8_ | | |

Target Behaviors	M	T	W	Th	F
1. Sits in seat	II	III	I	II	IIII
2. Finishes math in time		I		I	I
3. Asks to leave room	I	I		I	
4. Quiet during silent reading		I	I		I

Points from last week **4**

Total points **25**

BACK OF CARD

Operational definitions of target behaviors

1. _Keeps body firmly in seat with feet on floor for 15 minutes_

2. _Finishes math paper within time stated by teacher_

3. _Asks permission before leaving room_

4. _Remains quiet during silent reading period of 20 minutes_

Points needed for Big Reward _50_ Little Reward _5_

TYPE I
BEHAVIORAL RATING CARD (S)

FRONT OF CARD

Name of student _____ From _____ to _____					
Target Behaviors	M	T	W	Th	F
1.					
2.					
3.					
					Points from last week
4.					Total points

BACK OF CARD

Operational definitions of target behaviors

1. _____
   _____
2. _____
   _____
3. _____
   _____
4. _____
   _____

Points needed for Big Reward _____ Little Reward _____

SAMPLE TYPE II
BEHAVIORAL RATING CARD (S)

FRONT OF CARD

Name of student _Mike Lauder_   From _3/12_   to _3/16_

Subject Areas

Subject		M		T		W		Th		F
Science	1	✓	1	✓	1	✓	1		1	✓
	2	✓	2		2		2	✓	2	
	3		3	✓	3		3	✓	3	
Math	1	✓	1		1		1	✓	1	✓
	2		2	✓	2		2	✓	2	
	3		3		3		3	✓	3	
English	1	✓	1	✓	1	✓	1		1	✓
	2		2	✓	2		2		2	✓
	3		3	✓	3		3		3	✓
Gym	1	✓	1		1	✓	1		1	✓
	2		2		2		2		2	
	3		3		3		3		3	
History	1	✓	1		1		1	✓	1	
	2		2	✓	2		2		2	
	3		3		3		3	✓	3	

BACK OF CARD

Operational definitions of target behaviors

1. _Pays attention as measured by the correct_
   answer to a question randomly asked by teacher

2. _Hands in homework on time_

3. _Volunteers to answer a question in class_
   (one check per question volunteered for)

Points from last week _7_   Total points _36_

Points needed for Big Reward _60_   Little Reward _10_

TYPE II
BEHAVIORAL RATING CARD (S)

FRONT OF CARD

Name of student _____ From _____ to _____										
Subject Areas		M		T		W		Th		F
	1		1		1		1		1	
	2		2		2		2		2	
	3		3		3		3		3	
	1		1		1		1		1	
	2		2		2		2		2	
	3		3		3		3		3	
	1		1		1		1		1	
	2		2		2		2		2	
	3		3		3		3		3	
	1		1		1		1		1	
	2		2		2		2		2	
	3		3		3		3		3	
	1		1		1		1		1	
	2		2		2		2		2	
	3		3		3		3		3	

BACK OF CARD

Operational definitions of target behaviors

1. _____

_____

2. _____

_____

3. _____

_____

Points from last week _____ Total points _____

Points needed for Big Reward _____ Little Reward _____

GUIDELINES FOR PARENTAL DISCIPLINE

RATIONALE/PURPOSE

In teaching others to use behavioral techniques, specificity is important. Often parents have some idea that their behaviors may be part of the problem, but are at a loss to identify which ones are problematic and how those behaviors are contributing to the dilemma. They are especially unclear on how to correct the situation. A specific set of dos and don'ts generally is a good place to start in the parent teaching process. We have found that such a list gives parents something concrete by which to be guided.

ADMINISTRATION

The Guidelines are generally distributed and taught to parents or those in charge of a child's discipline by someone skilled in behavior modification and parent training.

GUIDELINES

1. The professional overseeing the use of the Guidelines should frequently and regularly review how successfully the parents are applying the discipline procedures.
2. If possible, both parents should be learning the Guidelines. A commitment from the parties involved should be established so the discipline of the child is done in a consistent manner.
3. Should one parent disagree with the Guidelines in general or with some items in particular, the professional might try spending more time on the groundwork. Then a step-by-step (or guideline-by-guideline) approach might be helpful. For example, if the mother feels she doesn't want to cooperate with the father on the Guidelines, perhaps she might agree to trying Guideline 1 for a day or a week.
4. Parents should be helped to understand that behavior change takes time. A shaping process occurs for their behavior as well as that of the child. They should be made aware that they will only gradually learn to change behavior. At first they may remember the appropriate guideline after the fact. In time and with practice this recognition will occur simultaneously with the child's behavior, and in the final stage they should be able to foresee behaviors and prepare to act accordingly.

USE OF THE INFORMATION

The professional disseminating the Guidelines for Parental Discipline should pick the appropriate time to teach this material. Often the discussion takes at least a 1-hour session to cover salient points and answer questions.

If the skills of the parents are in much need of revision and shaping, it may be wise to have them record the events that pertain to one or more of the Guidelines. For example, the parents might be instructed to write down the frequency and a brief description per occurrence of their violations of Guideline 1 (Never disagree about discipline in front of the children). As noted earlier, it may be wise to approach the Guidelines one by one in some cases.

COMPARISON TO OTHER FORMS

BEHAVIOR STATUS CHECKLIST (P): By identifying the components of the behavioral repertoire of the child as seen by the parents, the therapist can question the parents on how they deal with given behaviors and thus find out which areas of parenting need specific guidelines. Differences in handling of behaviors by different parents may also be noted (Guideline 4).

RESPONSE COST SURVEY SCHEDULE and GUIDELINES FOR TIME-OUT: The parents may find these forms helpful in setting up aversive consequences for specific behaviors (Guidelines 3–7).

REINFORCEMENT SURVEY SCHEDULES and PARENTS' AND CHILDREN'S REINFORCEMENT SURVEY SCHEDULE: These forms would be helpful to parents in establishing positive consequences for desirable behaviors (Guideline 11).

RECOMMENDED READINGS

Becker, W. C. *Parents are teachers: A child management program.* Champaign, Ill.: Research Press, 1971.

Berkowitz, B. P., & Graziano, A. M. Training parents as behavior therapists: A review. *Behaviour Research and Therapy,* 1972, *10,* 297–317.

Miller, W. H. *Systematic parent training: Procedures, cases and issues.* Champaign, Ill.: Research Press, 1975.

Patterson, G. R. *Living with children: New methods for parents and teachers* (Rev. ed.). Champaign, Ill.: Research Press, 1976.

Wahl, G., Johnson, S. M., Johansson, S., & Martin, S. An operant analysis of child-family interaction. *Behavior Therapy,* 1974, *5,* 64–78.

GUIDELINES FOR PARENTAL DISCIPLINE

1. Never disagree about discipline in front of the children.
2. Never give an order, request, or command without being able to enforce it at the time.
3. Be consistent, that is, reward or punish the same behavior in the same manner as much as possible.
4. Agree on what behavior is desirable and not desirable.
5. Agree on how to respond to undesirable behavior.
6. Make it as clear as possible what the child is to expect if he or she performs the undesirable behavior.
7. Make it very clear what the undesirable behavior is. It is not enough to say "Your room is messy." *Messy* should be specified in terms of exactly what is meant: "You've left dirty clothes on the floor, dirty plates on your desk, and your bed is not made."
8. Once you have stated your position and the child attacks that position, do not keep defending yourself. Just restate the position once more and then stop responding to the attacks.
9. Remember that your behavior serves as a model for your children's behavior.
10. If one of you is disciplining a child and the other enters the room, that other person should not step in on the argument in progress.
11. Reward desirable behavior as much as possible by verbal praise, touch, or something tangible such as a toy, food, or money.
12. Both of you should have an equal share in the responsibility of discipline as much as possible.

GUIDELINES FOR TIME-OUT

RATIONALE/PURPOSE

While most of the forms in this manual are related in some way to the assessment phase of behavior therapy, the Guidelines for Time-out form is to be used in the treatment phase. The Guidelines form will hopefully assist the therapist in two ways: first, it should provide a helpful tool in teaching others how to use the procedure, and second, it may provide a format for developing other useful handouts. When working with children, we have found that significant adults (parents, teachers, counselors) respond favorably when these forms are distributed and carefully explained.

ADMINISTRATION

The Guidelines can be distributed and taught to parents, school personnel, institutional personnel, and others living or working with children. It is recommended that a professional skilled in behavior modification oversee the use of this handout.

GUIDELINES

1. This handout should be carefully explained to those who will be implementing time-out. The professional involved should, on a frequent basis, review how the procedure is being applied and to what degree it is affecting the child's behavior.
2. It is advisable that the professional overseeing this procedure follow it from the behavioral analysis to the maintenance phase.
3. Other behavior modification principles and techniques may need to be explained during the program.
4. As in most behavior modification interventions, an effort should be made to include the use of positive reinforcement. In conjunction with the use of a punishment procedure such as time-out, Differential Reinforcement of Other Behavior (DRO), or the reinforcement of an incompatible behavior can be especially helpful. If an appropriate behavior that competes with the behavior to be eliminated is rewarded, the child is then taught what he should be doing instead of being taught only what he should not be doing.
5. As for all consequences, whether or not time-out is punitive in a given situation can only be determined by the effect the consequence has on the occurrence of the behavior. Time-out in some situations (not many) may increase the occurrence of the behavior.

USE OF THE INFORMATION

An ongoing collection of data is essential in the use of time-out, as with all behavior therapy. Before a time-out procedure is instituted, a behavioral analysis in which the target behavior is functionally defined and measured and in which the antecedents and consequences are determined should take place. This information is needed in order to decide if the time-out procedure is suited to the situation and behavior. The professional who is instructing parties applying time-out also should assess the program on a frequent and regular basis. If the behavior is not decreasing as expected, there may be some error in the use of time-out or time-out may not be an appropriate technique.

COMPARISON TO OTHER FORMS

BEHAVIOR RECORD FORM: This form can be useful in determining the behavioral analysis data needed before the intervention phase.

BEHAVIOR STATUS CHECKLIST (P) and SCHOOL BEHAVIOR STATUS CHECKLIST: The time-out procedure may be applied to a variety of behaviors that are viewed as problematic by those in the home or school. The Behavior Status Checklists are helpful in identifying which behaviors significant others view as maladaptive.

GUIDELINES FOR PARENTAL DISCIPLINE: The therapist may want to use Guidelines for Time-out to teach the time-out procedure to parents who need help in disciplining their children.

PROGRESS CHART: In setting up a contractual program time-out may be useful as the aversive consequence.

RECOMMENDED READINGS

Drabman, R. S., & Creedon, D. S. Marking time-out: A procedure for away-from-home disruptive behavior. *Child Behavior Therapy,* 1979, *1,* 99–104.

Leitenberg, H. (Ed.). *Handbook of behavior modification and behavior therapy.* Englewood Cliffs, N.J.: Prentice-Hall, 1976.

Marholin II, D. (Ed.). *Child behavior therapy.* New York: Gardner Press, 1978.

Miller, W. H. *Systematic parent training: Procedures, cases and issues.* Champaign, Ill.: Research Press, 1975.

Murray, M. E. Modified time-out procedures for controlling tantrum behaviors in public places. *Behavior Therapy,* 1976, *7,* 412–413.

Patterson, G. R. *Living with children: New methods for parents and teachers* (Rev. ed.). Champaign, Ill.: Research Press, 1976.

Sachs, D. A. The efficacy of time-out procedures in a variety of behavior problems. *Journal of Behavior Therapy and Experimental Psychiatry,* 1973, *4,* 237–242.

GUIDELINES FOR TIME-OUT

SPECIFIC GUIDELINES

1. *Purpose of time-out.* Time-out means time out from reinforcement. It is a procedure used to decrease undesirable behaviors. The main principle of this procedure is to ensure that the individual in time-out is not able to receive *any* reinforcement for a particular period of time.

2. *Time-out area.* The time-out area should be easily accessible, and in such a location that the child can be easily monitored while in time-out. For example, if most activity takes place on the first floor of the house, the time-out area should not be on an upper floor.

3. *Amount of time spent in time-out.* Generally, it is considered more effective to have short periods of time-out, for example, 5 to 10 minutes, than to have long periods, such as half an hour to an hour. The younger the child, the shorter the time-out should be. A 6-year-old child should probably receive about a 5-minute time-out; a 10-year-old child, a 10-minute time-out. A general guideline can be: 6–8 years of age, 5 minutes; 8–10 years of age, 10 minutes; 10–14 years of age, 10 to 20 minutes. Some parents have found it to be effective to double the time-out period for such offenses as hitting, severe temper tantrums, and destruction of property.

4. *Specifying target behaviors.* It is very important that the child be aware of the behaviors that are targeted for reduction. They should be very concretely defined; for example, hitting means striking someone else with the hand or an object, or coming home late means arriving home any time after 5:00 p.m.

5. *Procedures for time-out.* When a child is told to go into time-out, a parent should only say, "Time-out for . . ." and cite the particular offense. There should be no further discussion.

   While in time-out, the child should not be permitted to talk, and the parent should not communicate with the child in any way. The child also should not make noises in any way, such as mumbling or grumbling. He or she should not be allowed to play with any toy, to listen to the radio or stereo, watch television, or bang on the furniture. Any violation of time-out should result in automatic resetting of the clock for another time-out period.

   It is important that all members of the household be acquainted with the regulations for time-out, so that they will not interfere with the child in time-out in any way, for example, by turning on the radio.

   If the child resists by refusing to go to time-out, he or she should be told that unless he or she goes into time-out immediately, the time will be doubled. If the child still refuses, he or she should be carried bodily into the time-out area and told there will now be a triple time-out. Each time the child leaves the area, he or she should be forcibly put back and told that another time-out period has been added. If parents are consistent, even the most resistant child will walk immediately into time-out when told.

ADVANTAGES OF TIME-OUT

1. It is less aversive than other procedures, such as physical punishment.
2. It eliminates a lot of yelling and screaming on the part of the parents.
3. It increases the probability that parents are going to be consistent about what is going to be punished, when, and how.
4. The child learns to accept his or her own responsibility for undesirable behavior. The parents are not punishing the child; rather the child is punishing him or herself. The child should be repeatedly told that the parents did not put him or her in time-out, but that the child put him or herself in time-out.
5. The child more readily learns to discriminate which behaviors are acceptable and which are unacceptable.
6. The child begins to learn more self-control.

7. When the parents first institute time-out, they can keep a record of the number of time-outs per day and the nature of the offenses. These data can then be used in determining the effectiveness of the program and in providing information on the particular behaviors needing more behavioral analysis and treatment.

MOTIVATION ASSESSMENT OF PARENTS AND CHILDREN (T)

Motivation Assessment of Parents
Motivation Assessment of Children

RATIONALE/PURPOSE

The Motivation Assessment of Parents and Children provides the therapist with a means of evaluating the motivation of the parties involved in therapy. It aids the therapist in examining the therapeutic situation and in establishing goals for treatment in general. The form provides a quick method of measuring one facet of progress from week to week over a period of time. The components of cooperation and motivation are behaviorally defined.

ADMINISTRATION

This form is to be filled out by the therapist after interacting with the parent and/or child.

GUIDELINES

1. To improve the accuracy of the responses, this form should be filled out as close in time to the session as possible.
2. Percents have been established as part of this form to provide the therapist with a more accurate appraisal of frequency and duration.
3. The results may be graphed for a visual representation. In some cases the therapist may want to show the parent or child the forms or the graph to further reinforce the desired behaviors.

ITEM BREAKDOWN

MOTIVATION ASSESSMENT OF PARENTS

Number of questions: 11

Questions	Topic
1–3, 10	Verbal cooperation
4, 6, 7	Compliance with instructions
5, 9	Availability
8	Supportiveness
11	Other behaviors expressing motivation

MOTIVATION ASSESSMENT OF CHILDREN

Number of questions: 12

Questions	Topic
1–3, 6, 11	Verbal cooperation
4, 7, 9, 10	Compliance with instructions
8	Availability
5	Attentiveness
12	Other behaviors expressing motivation

USE OF THE INFORMATION

The information collected over a period of time allows the therapist to focus in on specific areas that may be reducing the effectiveness of therapy. Thus, the information for each question should be compiled and changes noted. If there has been no positive change in an area that is in need of change, then it may be time for the therapist to review the methods she is using. If several areas are not improving, the therapist and client may want to review the client's commitment to the therapeutic process.

COMPARISON TO OTHER FORMS

REINFORCEMENT SURVEY SCHEDULES and REINFORCEMENT MENU: If motivation is assessed as being low, the therapist should review these schedules. Perhaps the rewards being used for behavior change are not in fact reinforcing at this time.

SESSION REPORT: The Session Report, in conjunction with the Motivation Assessment forms, usually presents a complete picture of the therapy session.

RECOMMENDED READINGS

Goldfried, M. R., & Davison, G. C. *Clinical behavior therapy.* New York: Holt, Rinehart and Winston, 1976.
Kanfer, F. H., & Phillips, J. S. *Learning foundations of behavior therapy.* New York: Wiley, 1970.

MOTIVATION ASSESSMENT OF PARENTS (T)

Name of parent _____ Date _____

Name of child _____ Session no. _____

Name of therapist _____

Circle the number that best describes how often the parent performs each of the listed behaviors.

    1 — Not at all/0% of the time
    2 — A little/25% of the time
    3 — A fair amount/50% of the time
    4 — Much/75% of the time
    5 — Very much/close to 100% of the time

Behavior Occurs

1. States that he or she wants help for the child	1 2 3 4 5
2. Answers questions nonevasively	1 2 3 4 5
3. Answers questions fully	1 2 3 4 5
4. Consistently applys procedures taught	1 2 3 4 5
5. Shows up for appointments	1 2 3 4 5
6. Does homework assignments	1 2 3 4 5
7. Keeps records as required	1 2 3 4 5
8. Reinforces the therapist's work with the child	1 2 3 4 5
9. Is readily available by phone	1 2 3 4 5
10. Volunteers information about problems of interaction with the child	1 2 3 4 5

11. List any other significant behaviors performed by the parent related to motivation. _____

_____

_____

_____

MOTIVATION ASSESSMENT OF CHILDREN (T)

Name of child _____   Date _____

Age _____ Sex _____

School _____   Grade _____

Name of therapist _____   Session no. _____

Circle the number that best describes how often the child performs each of the listed behaviors.

          1 — Not at all/0% of the time
          2 — A little/25% of the time
          3 — A fair amount/50% of the time
          4 — Much/75% of the time
          5 — Very much/close to 100% of the time

	Behavior Occurs
1. States that he or she wants help in changing behavior	1 2 3 4 5
2. Answers questions nonevasively	1 2 3 4 5
3. Answers questions fully	1 2 3 4 5
4. Follows instructions	1 2 3 4 5
5. Is attentive	1 2 3 4 5
6. Initiates conversation	1 2 3 4 5
7. Cooperates with procedures	1 2 3 4 5
8. Shows up for appointments	1 2 3 4 5
9. Does homework assignments	1 2 3 4 5
10. Keeps records as required	1 2 3 4 5
11. Volunteers information concerning his or her problems even if embarrassing	1 2 3 4 5

12. List any other significant behaviors performed by the child related to motivation. _____

_____

_____

_____

RATIONALE/PURPOSE

The Progress Chart serves several useful purposes in the behavior change process: first, it provides an ongoing record of the target behavior; second, it involves the child or adolescent in the measurement of progress in a reinforcing way; third, it encourages parents to look positively at the child's or adolescent's behaviors; and fourth, it summarizes the components of the program. It is a contractual agreement in which the target behavior is functionally defined and the consequences of the behavior, both positive and negative, are stated clearly. The accumulation of stars, checks, or points provides a readily available visual representation of what is occurring. Often seeing progress in measurable terms serves to reinforce the desired behaviors of both parents and their children. The stars, checks, and points often become secondary or conditioned reinforcers and at some point may be used in the generalization process as the main reinforcers.

ADMINISTRATION

This form is to be filled out by the child or adolescent and the parent together. The child or adolescent places the star, check, or point in the appropriate place on the form while the parent looks on.

The negotiation of the chart should involve a third party who is designated as witness and facilitator. Should a problem arise after the contract is written, the parties involved should get together and renegotiate the contingencies.

GUIDELINES

1. Look at the Sample Progress Chart (C) on page 190.
    a. The number in the box in the upper left-hand corner, *Checks/stars from last week,* is the total number of checks or stars left over from the previous week.
    b. The child's name, the dates the chart spans, and the target behavior are to be written in the spaces across the top. If there is to be a negative consequence when the target behavior is not performed, state this consequence clearly in the line below the target behavior. The behavior being targeted should be clearly and specifically stated on each chart, even though it may remain the same for a number of weeks in a row. It should be brought to the child's attention each week.
    c. Three areas need to be completed in the *Reward Box.* First, the behavioral requirements for earning a check or star are written in the center. There is usually one check or point given for each performance of the behavior.

    To the left is the area for the *Little Reward.* This is a small reward to help the child maintain interest while she is working toward a larger one. The number of checks or stars total or in a row necessary to earn the Little Reward should be clearly established. It should be a small amount; for example, for remaining dry each night, two stars in a row might earn a half-hour of television beyond the usual bedtime or a half-hour of extra story time with dad. Since it is possible for a child to earn more than one Little Reward within a week, it may be helpful to specify several Little Rewards.

    To the right of the center is the area for the *Big Reward.* This is the main reward the child is working for. Again, the number of points total or in a row needed to earn the reward should be made clear. The amount of points should be large, but achievable; for example, if the target behavior is remaining dry all night, the child might have to earn 20 stars total to be able to buy a new tire for her bicycle. The Big Reward often carries over from the previous week.
    d. The check or star should be placed on the chart by the child as close in time to the behavior as possible, with the parent supportively watching and praising. Pairing rewards with praise often facilitates the generalization process.

e. In the lower right-hand corner is the *Total checks/stars* box. The number there indicates the total number of checks or stars earned to date. This should be filled in at the end of the week. To find the total, add the number from *Checks/stars from last week* to the number earned this week. If the child is ready to cash in checks or stars for the Big Reward, subtract the necessary amount; do *not* subtract any checks or stars for Little Rewards. This gives you the total. The total number should also be transferred to the *Checks/stars from last week* box on the new week's chart. A special time should be set aside for this particular step so the child's progress is noted and positively acknowledged.

2. Look at the Sample Progress Chart (A) on page 192.

   a. In the upper left-hand corner is the *Total points from last week* box. The number there is the total number of points left over from the previous week.

   b. The adolescent's name, the dates the chart spans, and the target behavior go in the spaces across the top. Even if it remains the same over several weeks, the target behavior should always be included.

   c. Three areas need to be filled in for the *Contract* box. The first is the *Short-Term Agreement* area. This is an agreement made between the parent and adolescent on the number of times and manner in which the behavior must be done if the adolescent is to earn a small reward. Such rewards should be contingent upon small amounts of behavior. For instance, if the targeted behavior is making the bed by a certain time each morning, the agreement might require that the adolescent make the bed by the expected time 3 days in a row in order to earn the privilege of having a friend stay overnight. Points are *not* subtracted from the total for small rewards. Negative consequences also can be stated in the Short-Term Agreement, as shown in the example.

   The second area is the *Long-Term Agreement* area. This agreement stipulates clearly what is expected from both parties in obtaining a large reward. The total number of points required to earn the reward should be noted and any stipulations on the behavior or reward should be outlined in the contract negotiations. For example, the adolescent might be required to make the bed by a certain time 100 times in order to get to go on a ski weekend. This kind of reward would require specifications such as how long the adolescent could be gone, where he would stay, and how much (if any) spending money would be included.

   The third area is the *Signatures* area. Here all parties involved must sign to confirm the agreement. The contract should be viewed as a binding agreement between the parent and the adolescent. Once the rewarder, i.e., the parent, has agreed to the contract, she should not hound the adolescent to perform or refrain from the target behavior. The Progress Chart should be completed in full each week and should act as a reminder to the parent and adolescent of the terms of the agreement.

   d. Points should be placed by the adolescent in the appropriate box as close in time as possible to the occurrence of the behavior. The parent, in monitoring the point placement, should pair praise with the earning of a point in most cases. There are some adolescents who do not respond well to praise from parents or do not appear to appreciate being complimented in the presence of others. Thus this decision should be made on an individual basis.

   e. The box in the lower right-hand corner, *Total points,* has the total number of points earned to date. To find this number, add the total points left over from last week (excluding those cashed in for large rewards) to the points earned this week. This gives you the total. This number should also be placed in the *Total points from last week* box on the next week's sheet.

3. Rewards should be varied so the child or adolescent doesn't tire of them.

4. Placing the chart in a visible spot sometimes enhances the behavior change process by acting as a reminder. However, some children and adolescents prefer to have this be a private project. Placement of the chart should be jointly negotiated by the parent and the child or adolescent.

5. Sometimes it is also helpful to graph the number of points accumulated for each week. Such a visual representation of progress can encourage both parents and children.

6. The general age range for the Progress Chart (C) is ages 3½ to 10. Some children on the younger end may not understand the process yet, and some on the older end may prefer the Progress Chart (A). The Progress Chart (A) usually works well for youngsters aged 11 to 18.

USE OF THE INFORMATION

The Progress Chart provides a record of the client's progress over a specified period of time for a given behavior. This record should be used to determine the efficacy of the program. A review of progress and of the rewards being used should be ongoing. When the behavior has become consistent for a long period of time, the reward agreements should be set up on an intermittent basis toward the goal of generalization of the behavior. (It goes beyond the scope of this manual to address generalization. The sources in the Recommended Readings section may be of assistance to the reader.)

COMPARISON TO OTHER FORMS

BEHAVIOR STATUS CHECKLIST: This form may be helpful in determining which behaviors are most appropriate to target.

GUIDELINES FOR TIME-OUT: A very effective combination in changing the negative behaviors of a child is setting up a positive component for the behaviors desired and utilizing time-out when the negative behaviors occur.

HOME VISIT OBSERVATION FORM: This form assists the therapist in identifying which behaviors should be targeted on the Progress Chart.

REINFORCEMENT SURVEY SCHEDULES: The items on these survey schedules provide possible positive consequences for behaviors to be learned or for the absence of behaviors to be eliminated.

RESPONSE COST SURVEY SCHEDULE: This schedule can provide possible negative consequences for behaviors to be eliminated or for the absence of behaviors to be learned.

SESSION REPORT: The therapist may want to attach a copy of the Progress Chart to the Session Report to which it corresponds.

RECOMMENDED READINGS

Blechman, E. A. The family contract game: A tool to teach interpersonal problem solving. *Family Co-ordinator*, 1974, *23*, 269–281.

Kazdin, A. E. *The token economy: A review and evaluation.* New York: Plenum, 1977.

Kazdin, A. E. *Behavior modification in applied settings* (Rev. ed.). Homewood, III.: Dorsey Press, 1980.

Marholin II, D. (Ed.). *Child behavior therapy.* New York: Gardner Press, 1978.

Stuart, R. B. Behavioral contracting with the families of delinquents. *Journal of Behavior Therapy and Experimental Psychiatry*, 1972, *3*, 161–169.

Wahler, R. G. Oppositional children: A quest for parental reinforcement control. *Journal of Applied Behavior Analysis,* 1969, *2*, 159–170.

Weathers, L., & Liberman, R. P. The family contracting exercise. *Journal of Behavior Therapy and Experimental Psychiatry*, 1975, *6*, 208–214.

SAMPLE PROGRESS CHART (C)

Checks/stars from last week

Name _Jill Stamp_   **From** _1/3_ **to** _1/9_

Behavior _Jill is to have completely dry pants at 7:00 a.m._

Negative consequence _If Jill is not dry at 7:00 a.m., she will take the sheets off the bed._

10

REWARD BOX

Little Reward

If Jill is dry for 2 days in a row, she will be allowed to stay up a half-hour later than usual.

1 star each dry day (dry at 7:00 a.m.)

Big Reward

When Jill earns 20 stars, she is entitled to one afternoon at the zoo with a friend of her choice.

M	T	W	Th	F	S	Su	
	★	★	★		★		
							Total checks /stars _14_

PROGRESS CHART (C)

Checks/stars
from last week

Name _____ From _____ to _____

Behavior _____

Negative consequence _____

_____

REWARD BOX	
Little Reward	Big Reward

M	T	W	Th	F	S	Su	
							Total checks /stars

SAMPLE PROGRESS CHART (A)

Total points from last week 17	Name _Matt Kuhn_	From _2/6_ to _2/13_
	Behavior _Matt will make his bed neatly as demonstrated by mother._	

CONTRACT

Short-Term Agreement

Matt will be allowed to have a friend spend the night on a
Friday or Saturday if his bed is made to parent specifications by
9:00 a.m. three mornings in a row. If Matt does not make his
bed twice during a week, he will be assigned an extra hour of
work on Saturday.

Long-Term Agreement

Matt will be able to go on a ski weekend with $20 spending
money and transportation provided by parents when he earns
100 points. Each point represents one instance of appropriate
bedmaking.

Signatures

Rewarder _Bob Kuhn_
Rewarder _Nancy Kuhn_
Rewardee _Matt Kuhn_
Witness _George Kent_

M	T	W	Th	F	S	Su
x		x	x	x		x

Total points 22

PROGRESS CHART (A)

| Total points from last week | Name _____ From _____ to _____ |
| Behavior _____ |

CONTRACT

Short-Term Agreement

_____

_____

_____

_____

_____

Signatures

Rewarder _____

Rewarder _____

Rewardee _____

Witness _____

Long-Term Agreement

_____

_____

_____

_____

M	T	W	Th	F	S	Su

Total points

SESSION REPORT (T)

RATIONALE/PURPOSE

As an ongoing record and reminder of the contents of the therapeutic session, the Session Report provides an easy, quick means of identifying the important facets of counseling and therapy. Particularly for the behavior therapist, it provides a way to record techniques used, problems worked on, and assignments given. It may also be of help to other therapists who utilize specific techniques and give ongoing homework assignments.

ADMINISTRATION

The Session Report is filled out by the therapist as soon after the session as possible. It is often difficult to take cogent notes and simultaneously pay attention to the client. Thus, filling out the Session Report after the appointment serves as a way of clearly summarizing the contents of therapy.

GUIDELINES

1. The therapist may wish to develop abbreviations for techniques and assignments.
2. Notes made under *General evaluation* should be detailed enough to help the therapist recall particular sessions.

USE OF THE INFORMATION

The information can be used as an indicator of progress from week to week and as an overview of sessions. The record of homework assignments also makes it easier to supervise outside progress.

COMPARISON TO OTHER FORMS

BEHAVIOR STATUS CHECKLIST and SCHOOL BEHAVIOR STATUS CHECKLIST: An ongoing comparison of the Behavior Status Checklists with the content of the therapeutic work should be made.

MOTIVATION ASSESSMENT OF PARENTS AND CHILDREN: The parents' and children's forms, used in conjunction with the Session Report, usually present a complete picture of the therapy session.

PROGRESS CHART: If a chart is being used, the therapist may wish to compare the behavior change in the home with the behavior change in therapy.

REINFORCEMENT SURVEY SCHEDULES: The Session Report gives some idea of the progress being made in therapy. To ensure progress, it is very important to continuously reassess the reinforcements being applied both in and outside of therapy.

RECOMMENDED READINGS

Ford, J. D. Therapeutic relationship in behavior therapy: An empirical analysis. *Journal of Consulting and Clinical Psychology*, 1978, *46*, 1302–1314.

O'Leary, K. D., Turkewitz, H., & Taffel, S. Parent and therapist evaluation of behavior therapy in a child psychological clinic. *Journal of Consulting and Clinical Psychology*, 1973, *41*, 279–283.

SESSION REPORT (T)

Client _____   Date _____

Therapist _____   Session no. _____

1. Was the client cooperative? _____

2. What techniques did you use? _____

_____

_____

_____

_____

_____

3. What special problems did the client report? _____

_____

_____

_____

_____

4. What problems were involved in administering the procedures? _____

_____

_____

_____

5. What were your recommendations and assignments? What forms are to be filled out? _____

_____

_____

_____

6. General evaluation _____

_____

_____

_____

_____

Bibliography

ASSESSMENT

Barlow, D. H. (Ed.). *Behavioral assessment of adult disorders.* New York: Guilford Press, 1981.

Baron, M. G., & Cautela, J. R. *Imagery assessment with normal and special needs children.* Paper presented at workshop during the annual meeting of the Association for the Advancement of Behavior Therapy, Toronto, November 1981.

Cautela, J. R. Behavior therapy and the need for behavioral assessment. *Psychotherapy: Theory, Research and Practice,* 1968, *5,* 175–179.

Cautela, J. R., & Brion-Meisels, L. A children's reinforcement survey schedule. *Psychological Reports,* 1979, *44,* 327–328.

Daley, M. F. The "reinforcement menu": Finding effective reinforcers. In E. J. Mash & L. G. Terdal (Eds.), *Behavior therapy assessment: Diagnosis, design and evaluation.* New York: Springer, 1976.

Liberman, R. P. *A guide to behavioral analysis and therapy.* Elmsford, N. Y.: Pergamon Press, 1972.

Mash, E. J., & Terdal, L. G. (Eds.). *Behavioral assessment of childhood disorders.* New York: Guilford Press, 1981.

Popovich, D. *A prescriptive behavioral checklist for the severely and profoundly retarded.* Baltimore: University Park Press, 1977.

Sulzer-Azaroff, B., & Mayer, G. R. *Applying behavior-analysis procedures with children and youth.* New York: Holt, Rinehart and Winston, 1977.

Walker, C. E., Hedberg, A., Clement, P. W., & Wright, L. Assessment. In *Clinical procedures for behavior therapy.* Englewood Cliffs, N. J.: Prentice-Hall, 1981.

Wolpe, J., & Lang, P. J. A fear survey schedule for use in behavior therapy. *Behaviour Research and Therapy,* 1964, *2,* 27–30.

GENERAL

Bandura, A. *Principles of behavior modification.* New York: Holt, Rinehart and Winston, 1969.

Craighead, W. E., Kazdin, A. E., & Mahoney, M. J. *Behavior modification: Principles, issues and applications* (2nd ed.). Boston: Houghton-Mifflin, 1981.

Fischer, J., & Gochros, H. L. *Planned behavior change: Behavior modification in social work.* New York: The Free Press, 1975.

Franks, C. M. (Series ed.). *Springer series in behavior modification: Theory/research/application.* New York: Springer, 1976.

Graziano, A. *Behavior therapy for children* (Vol. II). Chicago: Aldine, 1975.

Gross, A., & Drabman, R. Behavioral contrast and behavior therapy. *Behavior Therapy,* 1981, *12,* 231–246.

Kazdin, A. E. *Behavior modification in applied settings* (Rev. ed.). Homewood, Ill.: Dorsey Press, 1980.

Keller, F. S. *Learning: Reinforcement theory* (2nd ed.). New York: Random House, 1969.

Marholin II, D. (Ed.). *Child behavior therapy.* New York: Gardner Press, 1978.

Patterson, G. R. *Living with children: New methods for parents and teachers* (Rev. ed.). Champaign, Ill.: Research Press, 1976.

Skinner, B. F. *Science and human behavior.* New York: Macmillan, 1953.

Stahl, J., Fuller, E., Lefebvre, M., & Burchard, J. B. A youth center model for community-based intervention. Paper presented at the meeting of the American Psychological Association, New Orleans, August 1974.

Upper, D., & Ross, S. M. (Eds.). *Behavioral group therapy, 1979: An annual review.* Champaign, Ill.: Research Press, 1979.

——. *Behavioral group therapy, 1980: An annual review.* Champaign, Ill.: Research Press, 1980.

——. *Behavioral group therapy, 1981: An annual review.* Champaign, Ill.: Research Press, 1981.

SPECIFIC TECHNIQUES

Azrin, N. H., & Besalel, V. A. *How to use overcorrection (for misbehaviors and errors).* Lawrence, Kans.: H & H Enterprises, 1980.

——. *How to use positive practice.* Lawrence, Kans.: H & H Enterprises, 1980.

Bachrach, A. W., & Swindle, F. L. *Developmental therapy for young children with autistic characteristics.* Baltimore: University Park Press, 1978.

Baer, D. M. *How to plan for generalization.* Lawrence, Kans.: H & H Enterprises, 1980.

Cautela, J. R. Covert sensitization. *Psychological Reports,* 1967, *20,* 459–468.

————. Covert negative reinforcement. *Journal of Behavior Therapy and Experimental Psychiatry,* 1970, *1,* 273–278. (a)

————. Covert reinforcement. *Behavior Therapy,* 1970, *1,* 33–50. (b)

————. Covert extinction. *Behavior Therapy,* 1971, *2,* 192–200.

————. Covert response cost. *Psychotherapy: Theory, Research and Practice,* 1976, *13,* 397–404.

————. Behavioral treatment of elderly patients with depression. In J. F. Clarkin & H. Glazer (Eds.), *Depression: Behavioral and directive intervention strategies.* New York: Garland STPM Press, 1981. (a)

————. *Organic dysfunction survey schedules.* Champaign, Ill.: Research Press, 1981. (b)

Cautela, J. R., & Bennett, A. Covert conditioning. In R. Corsini (Ed.), *Handbook of innovative psychotherapies.* New York: Wiley, 1981.

Cautela, J. R., Flannery, R. B., & Hanley, S. Covert modeling: An experimental test. *Behavior Therapy,* 1974, *5,* 494–502.

Cautela, J. R., & Groden, J. *Relaxation: A comprehensive manual for adults, children, and children with special needs.* Champaign, Ill.: Research Press, 1978.

Hall, R. V., & Hall, M. C. *How to use planned ignoring (extinction).* Lawrence, Kans.: H & H Enterprises, 1980. (a)

————. *How to use systematic attention and approval.* Lawrence, Kans.: H & H Enterprises, 1980. (b)

Jacobson, E. *Progressive relaxation.* Chicago: University of Chicago Press, 1938.

Kazdin, A. E. Covert modeling, model similarity, and reduction of avoidance behavior. *Behavior Therapy,* 1974, *5,* 325–340.

————. *The token economy: A review and evaluation.* New York: Plenum, 1977.

Lovaas, O. I., Koegel, R., Simmons, J. Q., & Long, J. S. Some generalization and follow-up measures on autistic children in behavior therapy. *Journal of Applied Behavior Analysis,* 1973, *6,* 131–166.

Mash, E. J., Handy, L. C., & Hamerlynck, L. A. *Behavior modification approaches to parenting.* New York: Brunner/Mazel, 1976.

Miller, W. H. *Systematic parent training: Procedures, cases and issues.* Champaign, Ill.: Research Press, 1975.

Sloane, Jr., H. N. *Because I said so.* Fountain Valley, Calif.: How To Publications, 1976. (a)

————. *Dinner's ready.* Fountain Valley, Calif.: How To Publications, 1976. (b)

————. *No more whining.* Fountain Valley, Calif.: How To Publications, 1976. (c)

————. *Not 'til your room's clean.* Fountain Valley, Calif.: How To Publications, 1976. (d)

————. *Stop that fighting.* Fountain Valley, Calif.: How To Publications, 1976. (e)

Striefel, S. *How to teach through modeling and imitation.* Lawrence, Kans.: H & H Enterprises, 1980.

Thompson, T., & Grabowski, J. *Behavior modification of the mentally retarded* (2nd ed.). New York: Oxford University Press, 1977.

Upper, D., & Cautela, J. R. (Eds.). *Covert conditioning.* Elmsford, N. Y.: Pergamon Press, 1979.

Wolpe, J. *Psychotherapy by reciprocal inhibition.* Stanford, Calif.: Stanford University Press, 1958.

ABOUT THE AUTHORS

Joseph R. Cautela

Dr. Cautela is a licensed psychologist and a professor in the psychology department at Boston College. A past president of the Association for the Advancement of Behavior Therapy and a widely recognized expert in the field, he has published three books and has written over 80 articles on behavior therapy. Dr. Cautela has extensive experience in private practice and is a consultant to the Veteran's Administration Hospital in Brockton, Massachusetts, the Children's Hospital in Boston, and the Behavioral Development Center in Providence, Rhode Island. He directs the Behavior Therapy Institute in Sudbury, Massachusetts.

Julie Cautela

Ms. Cautela has dealt extensively with both children and adults in her professional career. Her teaching experience has spanned the Head Start, primary, and secondary levels and has included the teaching of English as a second language to adults and adolescents. Ms. Cautela now works at the Behavior Therapy Institute, where she utilizes her ability to work with all age groups in providing both career counseling and private therapy. She is particularly adept at relaxation techniques and has lectured on the subject.

Sharon Esonis

Ms. Esonis' professional career began with several years of teaching, both in Head Start and on a secondary level. More recently she spent 5 years as a school adjustment counselor, working extensively with children, parents, teachers, and social agencies. During this period Ms. Esonis developed a very successful group program for teaching behavior management skills to parents. Now at the Behavior Therapy Institute, she continues to organize these groups for parents of children of all ages, in addition to carrying out private therapy.